H. H.
Feb 1932.

WITHDRAWN

ENGLAND, THE UNKNOWN ISLE

Some English Opinions of

ENGLAND,
THE UNKNOWN ISLE

"An astonishingly good picture... accurate and discriminating."
—*The New Statesman.*

"Clear and intelligent. We congratulate the author on his capacity to penetrate beneath the surface in all the phenomena of English life that he studies."
—*The London Times Literary Supplement.*

"Thrilling because it is flattering, with stings in most of its tails."
—*The Nation.*

"Mr. Portheim's gifts of observation are acute. There are no dull pages in this book."—Harold Nicolson, in *The Daily Express.*

"A brilliant study of up-to-date England by a foreigner... Shrewd and witty judgment of places, men and things, likely to be widely discussed." —*Sunday Graphic.*

Published by
E. P. DUTTON & CO., INC.

ENGLAND, THE UNKNOWN ISLE

by
PAUL COHEN-PORTHEIM

Translated by Alan Harris

NEW YORK
E. P. DUTTON & CO., INC.

115435

ENGLAND, THE UNKNOWN ISLE, COPYRIGHT, 1931, BY E. P. DUTTON & CO., INC. : : ALL RIGHTS RESERVED : : PRINTED IN U.S.A.

FIRST PRINTING, JUL., 1931
SECOND PRINTING, OCT., 1931
THIRD PRINTING, DEC., 1931
FOURTH PRINTING, DEC., 1931

CONTENTS

CHAP.		PAGE
I.	Climate and Physical Features	7
II.	Saxon, Norman and Celt	17
III.	Historical Origins	29
IV.	English Traits	41
V.	Town and Country	60
VI.	London	73
VII.	Oxford and Cambridge	95
VIII.	Society	110
IX.	Political Policy	127
X.	The Foreigner in England	141
XI.	Art in England	149
XII.	English Literature	164
XIII.	The Theatre in England	184
XIV.	The Press	197
XV.	England and Europe	210
	Conclusion	222

I

CLIMATE AND PHYSICAL FEATURES

EVERY continent is an island ; why is every island not a continent ? In defiance of logic we have given the western end of the continent of Asia the status of a separate continent under the name of Europe, and equally illogically we count the British Isles as part of it. From the point of view of geography it is an absurd thing to do, but from the point of view of history it is justified ; for while Europe is not a geographical unity, it is— or was—a cultural unity, though with frontiers that are not quite easy to define. Politically speaking, the truth, first properly formulated by Coudenhove-Kalergi, is that the British Empire is a continent in itself ; when it comes to culture, on the other hand, that is not a satisfactory description, for the reason that it is culturally connected with the United States more closely than with the continent of Europe and much more closely than with those of the Colonies that have coloured populations. England is a phenomenon that needs a special terminology to describe it, and this difficulty in fitting it into any category is pre-eminently characteristic of the country and of its inhabitants' mentality ; as a result of this ambiguity the opposite of any pronouncement on their nature may be equally true from another point of view. Everything in England is a compromise, an affair of ' not only . . . but also,' ' on the one hand . . . on the other hand,' from which a mean results on which we have to try to put our fingers. The country, the climate, the people, their culture, their politics and their religion all share this characteristic, which is responsible for the fact that the British nation is the least understood and the most extensively misrepresented in the world.

In any case, however one characterizes Great Britain, it is a thing apart. The Frenchman or the German thinks of England as one of the countries of Europe—a false assumption which is generally fatal to his understanding of her. The Englishman speaks of 'England' in contrast to the Continent, which is what he understands by 'Europe'; all the countries and nations of Europe are to him a unity which does not include him. England is a thing apart.

The Continental instinctively conceives of England as an island up in the North, an *Ultima Thule*, with which ideas of cold, rain and fog are inseparably associated; actually, however, even in the matter of climate, that all-pervading factor, its position is peculiar. It is damper and foggier than more northerly countries such as the Scandinavian; on the other hand it is far warmer, thanks to the Gulf Stream, than parts of the mainland which lie to the South of it. Its climate, like everything else about it, is a compromise; the winter is not particularly cold—in the South-West snow is quite exceptional—the summer not particularly hot. The seasons are not divided off by hard lines, and one may equally easily find fires in the summer and a fireless room in the winter. Its only constant feature is its changeableness : 'We haven't a climate, we only have samples of weather,' runs an English saying. The island is constantly swept by varying winds, while cloud and sunshine, rain and mist follow each other in swift succession. (The fog of the big towns is a special phenomenon due to coal-smoke.) The climate and

CLIMATE AND PHYSICAL FEATURES

the weather are full of transitions and fine shades—the language has developed a number of untranslatable expressions to denote them—all free from exaggeration, intermediate and undramatic; the sun does not scorch you there nor the cold kill, neither does the rain come down like a cloud-burst. The English climate has the same antipathy to anything immoderate or extreme as its product the Englishman has; it is moody but not preposterous or impossible—in fact, ambiguous.

The landscape corresponds to the climate, on which it most immediately depends, and is characterized by gentle transitions and an absence of sharp contrasts. The Highlands and the South Coast are certainly very different, but the change from one to the other is a gradual one, compared with, say, the change from Brittany to Provence or from the Pyrenees to Andalusia. England has no high mountains and no extensive plains, just hills of varying height; though there are no big rivers or lakes or forests, it is extremely well watered and well wooded. Its scenery is pastoral, its predominating colour green. The traveller finds himself surrounded by green pasture-land full of cattle and sheep, with green hedges between the fields running up and down the slopes in gentle undulations, and splendid trees standing singly or in small clumps—individuals all; the forest and the avenue are equally un-English, the former because it is too primitive, the latter because it is too self-conscious. The whole country looks like a great park: where it is not industrial town, it is garden, and in spite of the incredible density of the population, the complete peace of the country begins where the last house of the town ends. There is no peasant class in England and indeed no agriculture to speak of; it is because three-quarters of its inhabitants live in towns that the countryside seems so uninhabited. The country is in reality, apart from the raising of cattle, a park or pleasaunce, meant just to be beautiful and peaceful, a big recreation-ground to play and walk about in. That is what the Englishman, with his idyllic conception of country life, means by 'the country' to which he is so passionately attached ; it has as little in common with that alternation of forest, heath and arable land which is the continental 'country' as the English town has with the continental town. The sea is never far away and the prodigiously long coast line provides examples of every kind of coastal scenery ; but here too moderation reigns—the scenery neither rising to the heights of the glacier-crowned fiords of Norway nor sinking to the monotonous flatness of Holland. On the South-West coast, which is warm and luxuriant, the laurel and the fuchsia, the rhododendron and the eucalyptus tree flourish in the valleys almost as well as in a hot-house, while on the top of the cliffs you get the heath characteristic of the North, making it a cross between the Mediterranean and Sweden ; and even the North-East coast is a long way off bareness. In fact, the South of England is only semi-southern, the North semi-northern. The variety of lighting and atmosphere is endless, and no other country can boast such a subtle gradation of tints except Holland, the only country which has produced a school of landscape painters to compare with the English. Small scattered villages, ancient churches and splendid country houses nestle in the background of green ; it would be hard to find a more perfect product of European civilization than the life of an English country house, which is the symbol of the English ideal—the maximum chance of development for the few, tempered by the idea that *noblesse oblige* and by the breadth of sympathy shown by the few in welcoming new elements into their ranks.

The English country is extremely civilized and, in its present form, man-made. It has no steppes, deserts, forests or inhospitable mountains, and nothing resembling the unlimited expanses of the East or the shapeless monotony of Russia ; on the other hand, it is equally far from the Mediterranean clearness and the sharp outline which we associate with classical art. Though man-made, it serves no practical end ; there has been no bringing of forests and waste land under cultivation, and it is 'useless' in the sense that a garden or a park is useless, i.e, it serves no purpose that can be positively expressed in terms of money. Oscar Wilde said that it was the essential nature of art to be 'perfectly useless' ; in England the country is also perfectly useless—in other words, deeply significant and important. It is a truly English compromise between nature and art. The English do not violate nature and force her to accept Man's will in geometrical forms ; they want her to have a natural effect, but to that end they improve her and make her habitable : gardening reaches its highest point in England and nowhere else is the longing for nature, the love of animals and growing things, so strong. The country is one great garden, to dwell in which is every Englishman's dream. He is in no sense a townsman, thereby standing in strong contrast to the Latin ; but yet he is a man of civilization, not a peasant. He clings to the idea of the self-contained house in its own ground, and his towns are a compromise, an endlessly extended congeries of small houses and often minute gardens, grouped round a densely crowded centre entirely given over to business. English art, whether painting or poetry, has its roots primarily in the countryside ; conversely, the creation of that countryside has been stimulated by the poets' vision of Arcadia.

Love of the country is the most fundamental thing about the English and can alone make their character and their history intelligible. The whole structure of their society is based on the fact that the ownership of land is the height of their ambition and, consequently, the landowner their ideal. Sport, too, is only comprehensible from this point of view—as primarily the natural occupation of the landowner, who has long ceased to be principally an agriculturalist; by riding and hunting, shooting, swimming and rowing on the land and water that belong to him, he has given rise to the conception of the sportsman as the typical aristocrat, the ideal to which everybody would like to rise.

Their games, too—tennis, golf, cricket and the rest— have their origins in the country, in country houses or villages, and are the invention of people who like the open air but, owing to the climate, have to keep moving if they are to enjoy it. The principal nurseries of athletics and games are the educational establishments of the well-to-do classes, from which they make their way right through the population; when they start turning into entertainments they lose their original point, becoming a profession for the players and a circus for the onlookers. It is a characteristic that English athleticism is only spreading all over Europe now that it has assumed this form—just the form which has lost every specifically English feature. Six-day races, boxing matches under arc lamps, hard-court tennis tournaments have really lost all connection with country life and the love of nature, but the same word 'sport' is used for *circenses* which have lost all connexion with the old meaning of the word. To be a 'sportsman' in the English use of the word means to have a sense of fairness and decency, to be generous in recognizing another's superiority and modest where the advantage is one's own, to be both a good winner and a good loser ; in present-day journalese 'sportsman' means a man who goes to race-meetings.

English sport, English art, English Society are all rooted in that peaceful green-turfed countryside with its gently undulating hills and lofty copses, its flocks and herds and pale scudding clouds, where light and weather are for ever changing and the hills undulate gently and nature is human, hospitable and amiable. But all round this Arcadia rages and swells the sea, so near that you can never forget about it, and this completely humanized, garden-like country is flanked by the waters that are inviolate as on the day they were created. It needed the co-operation of these two opposites to make England what it is. The land is idyllic but the sea stands for struggle and the broader horizon. The land by itself would have produced a race of peasants and landowners (the English character has, in fact, much that relates it to the Lower-Saxon), but the sea, by adding imagination and the spirit of adventure, has made sailors, traders, adventurers, conquerors, colonizers and empire-builders of them, and turned their little island into the mother-country of the Empire which this same sea holds together.

The view is constantly expressed both in speech and in print that England owes her undisturbed development to her position as an island, that she has been vouchsafed by nature a defence denied to countries with land frontiers, and that it is to this rather than to her own efforts that she owes her position in the world. But her history contradicts this view ; England has constantly been conquered from the Continent, and only achieved freedom after she had won the command of the sea for herself. The Romans conquered England ; so did the Danes, the Saxons and the Normans; and even after foreign invasions had ceased under Norman rule it was still centuries before England directed her gaze on to the sea and found her destiny there. For the time her fate was still tied up with that of the Continent, especially France ; only when she had given up her continental ambitions did she realize her true mission, the command of the sea. But so far from its falling into her lap without a struggle, it is in the struggle for it that her history in the last few centuries really consists. The British Empire sprang into existence on the ruins of the Spanish the day the Armada was defeated. If Philip II had been pleased by England and his English wife the history of the world would probably have taken a different aspect. When he came to England for his wedding, a tankard of the national drink, ale, was proffered to him as he landed, but after one sip he handed it back in horror. It may be that this first impression remained decisive and that the subsequent history is the history of a struggle between the Hop and the Vine, in which the Hop won, together with all its implications—Protestantism and Puritanism and Industrialism, right down to Henry Ford.

'God blew with His wind and they were scattered' says the inscription on the medals struck to commemorate the defeat of the Armada, which no doubt marks the beginning of the Englishman's convinced, instinctive belief in the mysterious and heaven-sent alliance between England, the command of the sea and the divine government of the universe, which even to-day has not left him. He can hardly conceive the idea of other nations' claiming the same right, when in reality, so he feels, they are only tolerated on the sea. 'Britannia rules the waves' is for him an article of faith, as for the pious Christian is the divinity of his Redeemer. The sea has made mystics of the English ; looking out from their green and well-kept park over the infinite ocean, they realize that one depends on the other, that the peace, wealth and fortune of their country were won by strife on those waters—with the help of Heaven ; for how could this little people on their little island have risen to be the greatest Power in the world without that ? After the Spanish pretensions, the Dutch; after Holland, France under Napoleon ; after him Germany under William II . . . there can be little doubt about the divine government of the universe.

Possibly the reason why England is so much less given to militarism than the rest of Europe is that the adventurous element in it has all been attracted to the sea. Its juvenile literature (and not only the juvenile) is good evidence for the strength of the spell cast by the sea : romantic stories of sailors and pirates are invariably popular ; pretty well every school-boy dreams of running away to sea, and these adventure-loving lads and young men grow into the discoverers and pioneers who make England an imperial nation. Only on rare occasions has she deliberately conquered or acquired new possessions ; in the majority of her extensions of her Empire the great adventurer comes first, and only at a much later stage does the government choose a good moment to avail itself of the situation he has created ; as late as the nineteenth century the activities of Cecil Rhodes paved the way for British supremacy in Africa in this fashion. First comes the pioneer or explorer who is drawn to adventure overseas and takes the risks ; after him comes the shrewd business man; and last of all the new territory is officially incorporated in some form or other in the sphere of British Influence.

Every Englishman has a bit of the countryman and a bit of the sailor in him ; apart from this combination there is no understanding his character, in which the former's prosaic tenacity and rooted conservatism are compounded with the latter's romantic love of adventure, boyishness and superstitiousness. I am not maintaining that this completely accounts for the English ; history and economic changes have played an important part ; but I do naintain that the basic features of their national character are only intelligible in the light of the climate, the nature of the country and the influence of the sea.

II

SAXON, NORMAN AND CELT

The English constitute the most admirable evidence both for and against the value of ethnological speculations: they are entirely of mixed race, but they have the strongest possible racial characteristics of their own. The Englishman is always recognized at once anywhere; yet from the point of view of ethnological theory there is no such thing as an English race. It is a mixture of the Celtic and various branches of the Teutonic races, possibly also of the Latin and Iberian. The same or something like it applies, with few exceptions, to all the nations of Europe, and the absurdity of ethnological theory lies in the identification of these original 'pure' races, the existence of which is after all only a theory, with any European people as it exists to-day (Latin France, Teutonic Germany etc.). Conversely the English are an example of the fact that when different 'races' mingle and for many centuries share the same climatic conditions and the same history, a race really does arise with both physical and mental features distinguishing it from others.

In addition to characteristic physical traits the Englishman has his own peculiar psychology, his peculiar ideals and attitude to life. It may be just the mixture of races that largely explains their ambiguity and comparative incomprehensibility, and it is necessary to investigate the character and history of each race separately in order to grasp its importance and the influence it has exercised and recognize the share it has had in forming the present-day English character. The aboriginal inhabitants (as far back as investigation has reached) were Celts, who survive pure-blooded to this day in Cornwall, Wales, Ireland and Scotland, the Bretons being their nearest kinsmen. In character and appearance they exhibit many features that generally pass for un-English. Frequently short and dark and of southern appearance, especially in Cornwall and Wales, they are mystical and consequently artistic, with a pronounced turn for religion.

The Welsh are one of the most musical of nations, and the Irish are among the chief representatives of Catholic mysticism, while Cornwall is the home of the legends that gathered round King Arthur, the epic of the Middle Ages. Ireland had its art and at any rate an ecclesiastical civilization when the German tribes were still barbarians, and the Danish and Saxon conquerors who pushed the aboriginals back into the hilly regions of the West probably destroyed a higher civilization which has left no traces. Stonehenge and the menhirs of Brittany confront us with an unsolved riddle; only in Wales do faint memories of the customs of the Druids survive: but the racial character has survived, and the fisher-folk of Cornwall are full of strange superstitions and religious fanaticism, in this case Protestant. People have tried to attribute their dark colouring to an admixture of Phœnician, or even Jewish, blood—the Phœnicians traded in Cornish tin—but just the same types are to be found in Wales, where the possibility of such admixture is excluded. The Welsh have the reputation of being sly and untruthful, which may also be regarded as the reverse side of the gift of imagination; the Greeks had the same reputation, and it is not such a far cry from the many-wiled Ulysses to Lloyd George. Wales is the land of choral singing and musical festivals; it is, besides, a great mining country, Cardiff being the chief English port for the export of coal, and it is highly characteristic that the most uncompromising and extreme Left Wing of Labour is to be found there and in the equally Celtic Glasgow district.

In Scotland too one sees mysticism and astuteness going hand in hand. Ossian's Highlands were the cradle of Romanticism and Scott one of its greatest prophets; on the other hand Britain's most efficient business brains, both in actual commerce and in politics, come from Scotland. The Scotsman is your real Puritan —the Scottish Sabbath is even to-day the terror of everyone of a different way of thinking; a fanatic like all Celts, he is quite as liable to carry his fanaticism into politics or money-making—his stinginess is proverbial—as into religion. The Scottish spirit is in many ways akin to that of the Old Testament, which is, no doubt, why the Puritanism that is founded on the study of the Bible has managed to take such deep root there.

But the most genuine Celts are, after all, the Irish, doubtless in consequence of their insular position. The Irishman is the most mystical, the most fanatical, the most ruled by his instincts and perhaps the most talented of the lot, and his country is the land of legend and poetry, reverie and devotion to the Church—in this case the Catholic Church, to which it has remained staunchly faithful. Ireland has given Great Britain many of her greatest poets and writers, but every Irishman has something of the poet, or at least of the visionary, in him. In art he is a man of fanatical devotions, either to his legends like Yeats or to satire like Swift or Shaw, or to extreme realism like James Joyce, and in politics the same, which has made Ireland a country of revolution and outrage. The only quality of his kinsmen that he lacks is the business instinct, no doubt because his country has given him little chance to develop such faculties. On the other hand the grandeur and solemnity of nature there have developed in him an inclination to a melancholy almost akin to that of the Slavs. The Irish folksongs are full of yearning, like the Russian; so is Irish scenery, quite unlike the well-fed look of the English country, and the Irish temperament is subject to the same sudden alternations of gloom and gaiety. The Irish are almost pure Celts; only in Ireland has every attempt at compromise proved abortive right down to the present day. In Cornwall, Wales and Scotland the Celtic element lends a distinct colour to a thoroughly British stock, while in Ireland there is a barrier between it and the others— though no doubt the misguided policy of her neighbour, prolonged into quite recent times, has done much to prevent the bridging of their differences.

Fanaticism in the spheres of religion and politics, mysticism, poetical and musical gifts—in a word, the strength of the irrational parts of human nature, are the most characteristic traits of the Celt. The Englishman has a lot of all those qualities in him; for though the Celtic nature can be seen unadulterated only in the above-mentioned parts of Great Britain, it is right through the country a real element in the compound called English. The English character contains Irish and Scottish elements, and Saxon and Norman ones too, as we shall see later; but there is just one element it has not got and that is the English: for 'English' means precisely the mixture and more or less successful synthesis of these characters. We have, however, advanced far enough to say that the widespread conception of the professional archæologists nobody took any interest in this discovery. The English have not a trace of that consciousness of Roman tradition and feeling of kinship with it which is such a vital thing for the Italians and the French. In many old English towns the plan of the Roman town is still recognizable, and the tracks of Roman cross-country roads still remain, but the characteristic Roman genius for keeping one's eye on the goal and taking the straightest line to it has nothing in common with the English character, which is its exact opposite.

The edifice that reared itself on the buried Celtic foundations was not Roman but Teutonic. It is impossible to disentangle the parts and ascribe them severally to the Danes, the Angles and the Saxons; even in England the civilization which they produced and its architectural remains, which are scarce and for the most part pretty barbarous and clumsy, are called Saxon. The Saxon supremacy was predominantly confined to the East and has left its mark in names like Essex, Sussex etc. The monuments of these centuries, which rank low in the scale of culture, may not be many, but they are of decisive importance; for they stamped the people with an indelible Teutonic stamp, and from that time onwards the race that inhabited the North-West of Germany also constituted, mixed with Celts, the population of England, and it continued to exhibit the same traits. They were a peasant people, with the qualities and failings of their kind; they were strong individualists too, in genuine Teutonic fashion, and their widely scattered homesteads did not readily combine to form a definite unity. Here we have the origin of the English country ideal—one's own little cottage standing in its own bit of ground, on which nobody can say one nay—expressed in the saying 'The Englishman's

Englishman as a dry, prosaic, rigid and dull business man is an indescribably superficial one, for this reason, if for no other, that deep in every Englishman there is a bit of the Celt.

It is difficult to estimate the influence exercised on England by the Roman Conquest. Even to-day the limits of Roman expansion are recognizable all over Europe ; the older civilization of the inhabitants of those territories which were included in it marks them off from their neighbours, as may be observed in Germany, and there is a certain kinship between the parts of the Empire now distributed among various States. But the ancient foundations are only still really clearly recognizable in the countries where the population is of Latin stock and Catholicism, the successor of the Roman Empire, has maintained its position. Neither is true of England. It was really hardly more than a remote military station and things never got as far as a real settlement, nor has Roman Catholicism been able to maintain its position there. People have often tried to find a parallel between the British Empire and the Roman and establish a similarity of character between the two races, but such parallels never get further than the surface. There is not a scrap of anything Roman about present-day England ; the pre-Roman and post-Roman influences have triumphed over the Roman. True, there are a great many Roman ruins and remains, but they are felt as something foreign. Only the other day the digging involved in the erection of some building led by chance to the discovery of Roman remains in the City of London which belong to the buildings of the Forum and prove that the great business centre stands exactly where the ancient one stood (the exact spot in question is occupied by the Bank of England) ; but it is no exaggeration to say that beyond one or two home is his castle.' Sturdy independence, reserve, a tendency to brood over things, religious feeling, love of nature, aversion from urban and commercial life, distrust of anything foreign or over-clever, complacent insularity, but also true simplicity, tenacity in clinging to inherited possessions and inherited tradition, liking for food and drink and the coarser material side of life, contempt for spiritual values except in so far as they go with ecclesiastical ones, respect and loyalty towards their hereditary leaders, a strong love of their own little homes—these are just the characteristic traits of the peasant everywhere, but particularly of the Teutonic peasant, and just the characteristics that are to be found even to-day in any average Englishman, in whom they are so familiar that people forget that they only constitute half the picture of his complex character.

The Anglo-Saxon character was the meeting-place of the mysticism and fanaticism of the Celt and a prosaic, exclusively practical quality of tenacious endurance, the forerunner of 'great practical England' and the coldly calculating middle-class tradesman, but of the old 'merrie England' too—Falstaff was a distinct Saxon. The Saxons invented English country life and the English inn and the English predilection for all things simple, straightforward, little and low-built; they shaped the English ideal of Home. Even to-day the Englishman builds his country house like a peasant's cottage ; he likes low rooms, small windows, big fireplaces and a great heavy roof—everything countrified in fact. His ideal house is a country cottage and even when it is in a town it pretends to be one. All showy and pretentious luxury he hates ; and the fact that the English home has no *salon* affects the whole of English taste, of which the keynotes are solidity and simplicity. The best material—wood, leather or cloth—is good enough and is never allowed to belie its real native qualities or conceal them beneath a mass of ornament. A piece of English mahogany or oak furniture, an English leather suit-case and an English suit are all expressive of the same spirit, the spirit of their Saxon forbears. The Saxon side of the Englishman—incidentally the one he most likes to show to the world—is exceedingly efficient, tough, solid and prosaic, narrow and unimaginative, and sound to the core ; it belongs to the England of beef and beer, of the comfortable, well-fed, self-assured, cool-tempered but domineering, obstinate and independent average man—the ideal John Bull.

John Bull is accepted as the typical Englishman, but he really only stands for one side of the English character, the Saxon-peasant side. Had the English remained what they were in Saxon times, an agricultural people, they would no doubt be a nation of John Bulls, but they are further from this primitive state than any other nation in Europe. Their country is a commercial and industrial country with a three-quarters urban population, and the centre of an Empire; and as they are to-day, they are no more just a variant species of the continental Germans, transplanted Lower Saxons or Friesians, than their country is adequately represented by the figure of worthy, limited John Bull. The Saxon element is only one element in their compound character.

The victory of the Normans over the Saxons in 1066 and the conquest of England meant the triumph of a higher civilization over a lower, of Chivalry over a primitive peasant-state, of the Middle Ages over the Dark Ages. The Normans were descendants of the Northern Vikings who had conquered Normandy, but

by the time they conquered England they had already
absorbed and assimilated the culture of the Continent.
They introduced the Feudal System, which, in many of
its characteristic phenomena, is still a living force in
England to-day. William the Conqueror divided the
land between his captains, earls and barons and created
an aristocracy based on the ownership of land. The
Normans and the Saxons intermingled without any
further big struggle; but the ruling class consisted of
Normans only, and henceforth Chivalry, ownership of
land, authority and superior culture go together as the
badge of a caste. This is the origin of the idea of the
Gentleman, which is still in England, and nowhere else,
an extremely vital and effective force. The gentleman
was originally really gentle, i.e. in comparison with the
uncouthness of the lower classes, sensitive and subtle,
with a superior education, a more perfect language,
and a higher conception of honour. It was his vocation
to rule, and it was natural that possessions, wealth, and
power should fall to his lot, because he really was a
superior creature.

The English mind is still dimly haunted by these
notions, only it has long been possessions and power in
themselves, apart from any justification, that make the
gentleman in the eyes of the People. In present-day
common speech a 'gentleman' means a man who has no
profession because it is not necessary for him to have
one; it is his business to hunt, go in for sport and
amuse himself, but he must not work; it is this, and
not his individual character, that is decisive. People
mistake the externals for the real thing, but they also
simply take the real thing for granted in all sorts of ways.
Even to-day the whole system of class divisions in
England, far more than in other countries, goes straight
back to the Middle Ages, which began with the

Norman Conquest. The highest class is still the wealthy landed aristocracy, which has never sunk to a mere court nobility as it did in France under Louis XIV or been deprived of its possessions as it was in the French Revolution ; it still consists, as it did in the past, of large landowners who are the successors of the feudal lords and still retain a trace of their old control over the administration of Justice and the Church as J.P.'s and patrons of livings, and are still local petty sovereigns and Lords Protectors in their way, while the country people are not independent peasant proprietors but mostly tenant farmers dependent on the landlord.

In the towns, among the trading and professional classes, there are unmistakable traces of the mediaeval guild system ; socially they rank lower than the landed gentry, but with great wealth or position it is possible for them to rise to their level, in which case they proceed to acquire land and adopt the way of life of the aristocracy, and their descendants in the second or third generation become aristocrats. It is the fact that the aristocracy, though it clings to its traditions, is yet always ready to take in new blood while, conversely, every Englishman's ambition is to become an aristocrat, that has enabled the class that was at the helm centuries ago to be there still in spite of every change. The Norman legacy to England was the aristocratic ideal ; at the same time the fact that this aristocracy was originally one of alien conquerors with a superior culture explains the almost mystical reverence which the ordinary Englishman still has towards it ; at the bottom of his heart he feels that the aristocracy are differently constituted and higher beings. Here, I think, are the real roots of English snobbery.

But this must not blind us to the Englishman's sturdy independence. Even William the Conqueror thought it better to conciliate the corporate feelings of the citizens of London and to confirm all their privileges. London had early developed a civic community, akin to those of Germany in the Middle Ages, which was well able to defend its rights. William built his fortress, the Tower, in front of the City gates and was only permitted to set foot in London with the permission of the City Fathers, and even to-day the King may only set foot in the confines of the City after the symbolic keys have been handed to him. The foundations of civic life are Saxon, just as those of the aristocracy and the Court, and with them the Church and the army, are Norman.

The many splendid architectural monuments of the Norman period are almost exclusively churches and castles. The style called Romanesque on the Continent is known in England as Norman, and it is a fact that 'Norman' buildings are nearer those of Normandy (e.g. Caen) than anything else; but from the earliest times they have a character of their own, explicable through the infusion of a Saxon element: they are heavier and more massive, less soaring and more tied to earth than French work of the same date which is akin to them, also less harmonious and consequently far more picturesque and romantic—a comparison which applies to nearly all later English architecture too. The finest specimen of Norman architecture in England is Durham Cathedral, set high up on its hill next to the Castle and commanding the whole neighbourhood.

With the Normans the era of invasions closed. The fusion of races and the process of unification were gradually completed, and the English people emerged with their peculiar character and civilization, which in the course of centuries took on those strongly marked features which distinguish it from all others to-day.

But to understand it, the first necessity is to bear in mind its original component parts, Celtic, Saxon and Norman. It is the only way to understand the endless contradictions that confront one at every step and to grasp how it is that this country is at once the most aristocratic and the most democratic in the world; why John Bull values the gentleman above everything else; how mediaeval chivalry and the commercial spirit confront one another in it; how the English Philistine is counterbalanced by the imaginative Englishman and the shopkeeper by the conqueror; how the romanticism of a Byron and the fanatical genius of a Turner or a Blake could spring from such a prosaic and matter-of-fact environment; how obstinate traditionalism and practical sense can be reconciled—in short, how this nation, so hard to understand, so full of contradictions and so complex, came to be what we see it is to-day.

III

HISTORICAL ORIGINS

One constantly sees it stated that the development of the English into a sea-faring and therefore, of course, commercial nation was the obvious consequence of their insular position, which sounds convincing and illuminating but does not accord with the facts of history. The English People and English history have been in existence since the eleventh century, but it is centuries before that history becomes the record of a sea-faring people or, for that matter, of a people in any way insular or isolated : in those centuries England was simply a component part of Europe, and its history and development follow ordinary European lines.

The religious revival that led to the Crusades succeeded in fashioning a united Europe, and the Gothic period which blossomed out of them has the same features in every European country. England took part in the Crusades and had its chivalry, its school of poetry and its Gothic cathedrals exactly like France or Germany ; and its ideals, way of life and ambitions were at this time absolutely those common to Europe in general. Naturally there was a national tinge about them : English Gothic, for instance, branched off from French, just as German did, and developed its own special characteristics ; it is less soaring and fanciful and more rectangular ; the churches run to length, with rectangular ends, and are less ornate ; their builders generally did not bother much about the porch, but as against that they concentrated on the perfection of the centre tower ; and so on. An English cathedral in the Decorated or Perpendicular style could not be mistaken for its counterpart in another country, though both belong to the same family ; but the word 'Gothic' always calls up the same picture, whether the country is England or another, as does the ideal of Chivalry with all that it implies. In contrast to that the concept 'Renaissance,' a few centuries later in date, has quite a different content according as it applies to Italy, Germany or England.

While it would be superfluous in this context to attempt a picture of the Gothic age and to investigate its blend of religious fervour, scholastic thought, love-cult and Chivalry, attention must nevertheless be called to the fact that it left a particularly deep and lasting mark on England. In the home of Gothic, France, the Classical style had a second innings, but in predominantly Teutonic England, as in Germany, this was not the case. When a Frenchman wants to get back to his past, his tradition, he gravitates towards the Classical; but England's Classical style is the Gothic. As a matter of fact Gothic never disappeared entirely, and the nineteenth century actually brought a Gothic Revival ; the English regard it as their national style, and not only in the sphere of architecture ; for the Gothic ideal never quite lost its hold on the English spirit. The present-day Englishman's conception of honour and decency are based on ideas of Chivalry linked with Christianity. The obligation to help the weaker side, to be magnanimous towards the vanquished, to fight with equal weapons—all that the Englishman to-day understands by 'fair play'—are of Gothic and chivalric origin : to the Ancient World or the Italians of the Renaissance, for instance, such obligations would have been quite meaningless. Consideration for the weak, for women and children, is a particularly English trait, which comes from mediaeval Christianity.

Altogether Christianity has preserved far more of its mediaeval significance in England than in other countries ; it has hardly recovered anywhere on the Continent since the Renaissance Even now Christianity and Church-going and religious questions play an exceedingly important part in English life ; moreover the conception which England has developed of the Lady (a quite untranslatable word) is absolutely determined by mediaeval notions. The conception is a very important one, because the Englishman's whole ideal of womanhood and his attitude to women altogether have been affected by it. The Lady stands on the pedestal on to which the Troubadours lifted her. In relation to the coarse male she is a superior, delicate being, a stranger to the ways of the world, modest and retiring ; a mere word may easily be enough to upset her, and an Englishman who swears like a trooper in the company of his own sex would consider it the height of ill-bred coarseness to do so in the presence of ladies. A lady is an innocent, soft-hearted creature who has no notion of the wickedness of the world and must come into contact with nothing low. She is an ideal ; in other words, she does not exist and probably never did ; she is in any case unfit for life and, if she did exist, would drive any man to distraction in five minutes ; yet she has remained the English ideal woman. English art has created no figure of the type of Manon Lescaut, Carmen or Marguerite Gauthier ; instead it has produced Rossetti's Blessed Damozel, Thackeray's Amelia and Shakespear's Cordelia. The Woman Pure and Undefiled (e.g. Lady Godiva) and the persecuted fair-haired Innocent are the Englishman's favourite female characters, and the innocent fair-haired heroine of Hollywood is the direct descendant of the mediaeval Lady. What other nations regard as English (or American) hypocrisy is largely founded on the blatant contrast between the ideal and the reality; the fiction is to be kept up, and the women play the part in which the men most enjoy seeing them, till they both end by believing in it because they want to believe in it.

The ideals of the Gothic Middle Ages are still alive in England, and the most solemn occasions are marked by mediaeval ceremonies. The Houses of Parliament are Gothic, and it is in the Gothic Abbey of Westminster next door that the King has received his crown, seated on a gilded throne in mediaeval robes, ever since mediaeval times; the older Universities, and many of their customs too, are mediaeval; the Law Courts are Gothic, and so is much legal language; the Guildhall is Gothic, likewise the office of Lord Mayor, which dates from the Middle Ages. Gothic was the first really English style, and the conception of life it represents is still the basis of English life to-day.

The age of the Crusades and a united Europe was followed by the period of the Hundred Years' War between England and France, when the English kings, whose origins were continental, were out for conquests and possessions on the Continent, and both the people and their rulers were still far from any idea of the sea and sea-power. It was still in Europe that England was seeking her destiny; she was a piece of Europe like any other country and not a particularly important one at that, and her kings played their small subsidiary parts in the European drama in which the Pope and the Emperor were the protagonists. Not till she had finally retired from France, renounced the hope of continental conquests and withdrawn to her island did

England begin to have a position of her own. Her renunciation was the beginning of her greatness, and that involved development away from Europe and withdrawal from the Continent.

The quarrels by which Europe was torn to pieces during the succeeding centuries had increasingly little effect on England, and the Holy Roman Empire and its struggle with the papal power were no business of hers. Then came the break with Rome in the reign of Henry VIII; and after long struggles England found her solution for the problem of the Church and its relation to the State in the co-operation of the two by a truly English compromise. Hence she was hardly involved at all in the Thirty Years' War which devastated Europe, and in this period devoted herself to home affairs and her own development, in which her isolation gave her the start of the Continent: true she had her civil wars, but their net result was an increase in the power and unity of the kingdom. The reign of Elizabeth saw England in full bloom; the arts and sciences were flourishing—it was the time of Shakespear and Bacon—and fugitives from the Continent were laying the foundations of the textile trades, while commerce and prosperity increased. Then came the decisive day in English History, the day on which the Armada was defeated.

The discovery of America had entirely changed England's geographical position. So far she had been an appendage of Europe, a last outpost; now she lay between two continents, not dependent on either but connected with both. The struggle with Spain revealed to her both the danger and the advantage of being an island, and when she inherited Spain's sea-power she came to understand its significance. The sea, in opening the gates of the world to England, made her realize for the first time that shipping and sea-power were her vocation and that she had a mission to fulfil : henceforward English statesmanship is in reality concerned with only one object, namely sea-power, compared with which no other question counts at all. For the moment, however, there were still domestic problems to be solved : the accession of the Stuarts to the throne did at last bring with it the Union of Scotland and England, but the Stuart Kings failed to understand the nature of the English, their passion for liberty and their Protestantism. The struggle of Cromwell and the Puritans against Charles I and his Cavaliers is significant in more ways than one, and Cromwell's victory and the execution of Charles were of far-reaching importance to the whole world ; with Charles the Divine Right of Kings received its death blow, when Parliament, his subjects, executed him and no punishment from Heaven smote them. This is the point where feudalism ends and modern democracy begins. The ensuing struggles led to the permanent triumph of the elected representatives of the people over the King, the army and the Church, and the chief problems that were subsequently solved by France in the eighteenth century and not till the nineteenth or twentieth by the rest of Europe, were settled in England as early as this. On the other hand, the fact that the Continent remained unaffected by this revolution shows how remote from Europe England had already become.

Finally, there is also a purely domestic aspect to this struggle. It was a struggle between two strains in English life that have never become completely fused, and perhaps never will—the popular, Saxon, peasant strain, narrow, obstinate, honest and strictly moral, which found its embodiment in Puritanism and its symbolic figure in Cromwell ; and the Norman-French strain of feudal Chivalry, cultured, diplomatic, aristocratic, free from moral prejudices, and Catholic (subsequently High Church), which expressed itself in the Cavaliers and the fascinating appearance of Charles I as Van Dyck has handed it down to us. Since that time the two tendencies have fought each other with varying fortune. The Puritan victory was followed by the restoration of the Stuarts; after their fall came the triumph of Protestantism and the middle classes under William of Orange; in the nineteenth century the Regency was 'Norman,' the reign of Queen Victoria 'Saxon,' but the latter lasted so excessively long that the foreigner's conception of England has become exclusively 'Saxon,' all the other elements being consigned to oblivion. Thus the Restoration, for example, with its unbridled licentiousness and its often incredible coarse literature, and the Court of Charles II, dominated by the King's mistresses, to whom so many English ducal houses owe their titles, are incomprehensible to the outsider who only has a superficial acquaintance with England, because they are so far removed from the hypocrisy, cant, moral earnestness, sabbatarianism, commercial spirit and lack of imagination which are inseparable in his mind from the idea of England. But Shakespear and Swift, Byron and Turner, Hogarth and Blake are just as impossible to fit into this conception, which, though not wholly false, is misleading through its one-sidedness.

With William of Orange the puritanical Saxon element gained an important, though little noticed, ally in the Dutch influence, which was in many ways akin to it. England was the heir of Holland, and not only of her sea-power, the destruction of which followed that of Spain's, but of her civilization. At a time when France was still completely dominated by the Court, in the great days of Versailles, and the Restoration was enjoying its temporary triumph in England, Holland had developed a culture of its own which was completely *bourgeois*. Her towns, especially Amsterdam, had become important centres of art and culture, just as other great seaports and commercial towns like Venice or Bruges had done in the past, and they had developed an architecture, an art and a style of domestic life all their own and unknown —as yet—in the rest of Europe. A wealthy *bourgeoisie* had here worked out for itself a form of its own to express its culture. Their houses were generally self-contained ; pressure of space in the towns necessitated their being narrow and rather high, and they were simple, unobtrusive and well proportioned. Gardening and its associated crafts were brought to the highest pitch of perfection ; their furniture was dark in colour and made of the best materials, with a *bourgeois* solidity about it ; and their clothes were of good sound cloth—not silk, which is appropriate to Courts. Their art is a reflection of this *bourgeois* life : they produced no frescoes and no ecclesiastical or court painting ; their line was portraits and landscapes of a moderate size suited to the walls of their patrician houses. It is a *bourgeois* art, even if a genius like Rembrandt does break through its limitations, without rhetoric, pomp or heroic sweep, a loving portrayal of every-day things seen in the light of every-day life.

This description of Dutch civilization in the seventeenth century also applies in its entirety to England in the eighteenth century and later. The typical London house resembles the brick houses of Holland, and eighteenth-century English furniture derives straight from the Dutch ; in fact the whole English tradition of comfort, solidity, and cosiness in the home, as far as town houses are concerned, came from Holland ; it produced houses for men of substance and not palaces. Together with gardening, the English took over the tradition of Dutch painting, and the work of the English School which arose at this time is a continuation of the Dutch ; Crome and Constable were the successors of Ruysdael and Hobbema, Hogarth was a second Teniers, and the great English portrait painters would be unthinkable apart from Franz Hals and Rembrandt, as they would also be apart from the Venetians. Taken as a whole their civilization has two characteristic 'notes' ; it is *bourgeois* and it is Protestant. It lacks the magnificence of the wide sweep and the big canvas ; it is neither erotic nor fanatical, nor has it a trace of mysticism in it ; but within its rather narrow limits it is perfect. It expresses the spirit of a proud, class-conscious *bourgeoisie*, such as was not as yet to be found in the countries where civilization was dependent on the Court; when it did develop in other countries, this type of civilization spread from England over the whole of Northern Europe and America, and in the nineteenth century became the dominant type, with the middle class at the height of its power and the Anglo-Saxon Protestant countries on top. The Latin countries were the least affected by it, but they forfeited their cultural supremacy.

The growing importance of the middle class brought with it a change in the character of the English aristocracy, which chose the right moment for every compromise, as we shall find it doing again so often later. Life at Court was simplified, and the nobility took to living, at least in town, in just the same way as the rich business-man. The latter had not yet worked his way into aristocratic circles, but the time was soon coming when he would ; for the moment it was literature that the middle classes invaded, the result being the English novel, in which, as in Dutch painting, the Gods, Heroes, kings and knights of earlier poetry gave place to ordinary human beings like Tom Jones, the Vicar of Wakefield, Tristram Shandy and the rest. The novel of middle class life, the first real novel in the modern sense of the word, originated in England as the expression of an individualistic Protestant civilization and was taken as a model by the rest of Europe. Thus did England repay a thousand-fold in the eighteenth century what it had borrowed from the Continent. Nor does this apply only to Art ; all those free institutions which England won through centuries of struggle became a model to the Continent : parliamentary government, a broad franchise, freedom of the Press, religious toleration, equality before the law—all these demands were first set forth by Voltaire and Montesquieu after they had lived in England, and then taken over by the French Revolution, so that since the eighteenth century the influence of England on the Continent has been much stronger than that of the Continent on England.

England took very little part in the wars in which the Continent was constantly involved. She prevented any great Power from establishing itself on the Flanders coast and fought against every country that attained, or looked as if it might attain, a position of predominance in Europe. Throughout the centuries she has known only one policy towards Europe, namely the maintenance of the Balance of Power, which prevented the formation of a coalition against her ; interests of her own in Europe she had none. Meantime she was conquering the world. The United States did, it is true, break loose from their mother country, but she retained Canada, acquired Gibraltar, on which her position in the Mediterranean depends, and, most important of all, gradually got possession of the whole of India. Having become the first sea-Power in the world, she waged war against Napoleon with unwearying tenacity, and English sea-power was the rock on which he split. The defeat of the Armada received its confirmation at Trafalgar; England proceeded to seize Malta, extend her Empire in India and Australia and add to it New Zealand and various key positions in China.

It was the dawn of the age of inventions, in which railways, steamships, coal and Industry revolutionized the world; England was there far ahead of all other countries, and the nineteenth century saw her first in sea-power, first in commerce, first in Industry, and the financial centre of the world as well. Realizing that she had become a continent in herself, she began for the first time to draw the threads of her Empire systematically together: Queen Victoria had herself proclaimed Empress of India, British power spread over Africa from Egypt to the Cape, and the great scheme of the Cape to Cairo railway was put in hand. The World War, in which England was once again fighting against the supremacy of a continental country and a fleet that looked menacing, and defending the Flanders coast, brought her Mesopotamia, a Protectorate over Palestine, and Iraq—almost the overland route to India. To-day, with the area of the British Empire greater than it has ever been—the British flag flies over a quarter of the surface of the globe and a quarter of its inhabitants—the Continent of Europe and its problems have long sunk into the position of secondary interests. Great Britain is the chief Mohammedan power; her centre of gravity is in the Indian Ocean; and Africa is the scene of her preparations for her future. She is a new and unprecedented political entity with its own peculiar policy and methods and its own future.

The Englishman of to-day is pre-eminently and *par*

excellence the colonizing White. As the centre of gravity of the Empire shifts daily further towards the circumference, the mother country is declining in importance ; her agriculture was finished long ago, and 'merrie England,' little but happy, has long been dead, while her Industry and trade are in a chronic state of crisis, surrounded by competitors who have arisen on every side and long ago out-distanced by the United States. Superficial observers regard England as out of date and reactionary, left behind in the race, in the grip of a decline ; but they are forgetting the British Empire, forgetting, above all, the British spirit. England has succeeded in making a spiritual conquest of her colonies (and other places too) ; the tie that binds them to her is far more spiritual than political, and consequently unbreakable. English customs, habits and ideals and the English language are supreme over half the globe ; but the wonderful little island still stands at the centre of it all, mother, some day perhaps it will be great-grandmother, of the family, with her memories that stretch so far back into the past and her ancient traditions, so full of contradictions, that have kept their vitality even in the age of Americanization, capitalism and Bolshevism. This England and the English of to-day, the figure they cut in the world, their lives, ideas and activities, are of the greatest possible consequence for the whole human race.

IV

ENGLISH TRAITS

PERHAPS it is always a mistake to try to reduce a whole nation to a common denominator, to label the Spaniards 'proud' or the Dutch 'phlegmatic,' for instance. Any such simple arrangement is bound to be absurd on account of its very simplicity; yet every nation has its several characteristic traits which in combination do form a general picture even if not an unambiguous one. The English have many peculiar characteristics and ideals, many of them peculiar to themselves, about which there is no doubt. Their ideal of character is the ideal of Repression. The nations of Europe may be divided into two types, those for whom the ideal is Expression and those to whom it is Repression. The Latins and the Slavs belong to the 'expressionist' type; determined really to 'live' their lives, they yield to their emotions and give outward expression to them; when they love or hate, feel happy or sad, they consider it the right thing to yield to these emotions and, so to speak, enjoy their flavour to the full. In doing this the Latin shows moderation and the Slav shows none, while the Englishman avoids it as far as he can, and the German oscillates between the two ideals. To one type the suppression of the emotions seems unnatural and gives a feeling of hypocrisy; the other type regards the uncontrolled expression of emotion as undignified, ill-bred, vulgar, almost bestial.

The English have opted for self-control invariable

and absolute, and for the repression, if not of emotion, certainly of its expression, to a degree only equalled by the Chinese and the Japanese. The English mask of immobility is first cousin to the Oriental's smile that must never be taken off under any circumstances in dealing with the outside world. Among the English all character training begins with the rule 'Never lose your temper'; whether you are pleased or annoyed, lucky or unlucky, preserve at least the appearance of equanimity and, if you can manage it, the reality. The First Commandment is : Control thyself. Lack of control bespeaks the animal, and the more controlled a man is the higher he stands ; a gentleman always keeps control of himself, and whether it is over sport or politics or business, neither victory nor defeat, neither good luck nor bad, disturbs his composure. The Englishman's view that all excess of emotion is absurd and undignified makes him misjudge foreigners (especially Southerners) and them him ; they mistake the mask for the face, and even when they recognize it as such, fail to understand the grounds for its use.

The English ideal of Repression is to blame for the wrongness of the judgments which are passed on England ; yet it is not improbable that with the extensive spread of games it will triumph on the Continent. Even in Latin countries tears of joy do not run down the cheeks of the winner in a tennis tournament, nor does the loser indulge in gestures of despair ; and one can hardly imagine a Dostoevsky character in a motor race or a boxing match. This athletic ideal easily gets transferred to life in general, and the man to whom the curbing of his emotions is the main thing in life is not going to indulge in continual self-analysis and so attach an exaggerated importance to his feelings. Besides, the Englishman is the least analytical of men ; about the feelings that he refuses to show he does not think much either, and excessive pre-occupation with one's own ego and in general all brooding over things strike him as 'unhealthy,' which is for him a serious term of reproach, and one to which nearly all psychology is, in his view, open. In these matters he is entirely irrationalistic, far too much of a man of action to bother with psychology ; Hamlet is a thoroughly un-English character.

It is, however, a great mistake to suppose that he is really as cold and unimpassioned as he makes himself out, and one has only to observe the lower classes to become convinced of the opposite. Being less severely repressed and not dominated by the fear of being 'vulgar' they reveal the great capacity for emotion that the English character has. The English taken as a whole make, for instance, the most enthusiastic audiences in Europe, not even excluding the Italians ; the enthusiasm of the spectators at any big sporting event is altogether unsurpassable, and a London crowd on a holiday is incredibly noisy, jolly and emotional. It is just because the Englishman is a man of very strong impulses that his education aims at subduing them, and because the unregenerate savage within him is still pretty strong he keeps him chained up. The unsophisticated Englishman has a lot of the Man with the Big Stick in him, which makes it all the more remarkable that this element so seldom comes to the surface ; the fact that the adjective 'barbarous' and the noun 'Englishman' will not go together proves that for him, in any case, his ideal of education has been the right one.

The passion for liberty and the inclination to conventionality are inextricably connected in the English. Absolute liberty of the individual is impossible in any society, being the same as anarchy; liberty is only possible within a framework of laws, and English liberty consists in imposing these laws on oneself. They are the conventions, obedience to which the Englishman demands of himself and his neighbour, and they are just as binding as the rules of a game, no game being possible without rules; whether it is a matter of bridge or tennis, politics or social life, if you want to take part in the game you must follow the rules, and anyone who is ignorant of them or disregards them is an 'outsider.' No one in the world is more tolerant than the Englishman as long as the prescribed forms are preserved; he bothers very little about his neighbours, and even within the family there is a very high degree of individual liberty; he does not inquire, and far prefers not to know, what other people are up to. He does not want to be forced to take cognizance of his neighbours' weaknesses; the latter is welcome to break every law on the Statute Book—that is his own business; but he is under an obligation to society not to give himself away, because in so doing he gives away Society.

There you have both the lighter and the darker side of English Cant and Hypocrisy. It is, at bottom, simply the extension of the standards which professional honour demands in certain circles in other countries too to large sections of the population, right down to the lower middle classes. It is precisely the middle classes, the great numbers and importance of which in England cannot be insisted on too often, that have the deepest reverence for the innumerable conventions. The upper classes take them with a grain of salt, knowing well that they are worthless in themselves but make life ever so much easier; nor do they cause much anxious thought to the lower classes, who do not bother their heads about them. In short, the upper classes make use of the

rules of the game, the middle classes regard them with
veneration, and the lower classes ignore them; but they
stump most foreigners, who fail to grasp the importance
attached to them and cannot understand that internal
freedom can very well be reconciled with an external
compulsion of one's own choosing.

The Englishman himself knows that following external
rules does not represent the highest ethical ideal, but he
argues as follows: 'even if one doesn't live up to the
ideal, still it is one's duty to go on as if one did; if one
isn't a decent sort of person underneath, one must at
least behave decently.' This may be hypocrisy, but it
succeeds in making decent behaviour generally compulsory. If English social, political and business life
exhibits that decency which makes it an object of constant and justifiable envy, that is to be put down to
education in the strict observance of forms which,
though external in their manifestations, demand to be
valued as symbols. When we get into our party clothes
we put on our party manners and party conversation
with them. The Englishman and his wife who make
a daily practice of this even when they are alone are at
first sight merely following what may look like a silly
convention; but thanks to it they treat each other
with the consideration, courtesy and amiability which,
without these external formalities, only too easily disappear
from daily life only to be brought out in the presence
of visitors. Every closed social corporation naturally
develops its forms and ceremonies for the simple reason
that they hold it together, and the older the tradition
the stricter its forms; hence their greatest strictness
in the oldest institutions and social classes—the Church,
the army and the nobility. What we see in England is
simply the extension of many of the rules that in other
countries are only valid and binding for the 'highest'

classes to wide sections of the nation as a whole. In
England the so-called aristocratic ideal is the ideal of
the great mass of the people : *noblesse oblige* and,
conversely, carrying out one's obligations ennobles.

Traces of this outlook are to be met with everywhere
in the daily life of England. In no other country are
there so few official regulations, so little that one 'must'
or 'must not' do. The laws are unwritten, and custom
and usage are binding ; the Englishman automatically
keeps to the proper side of the road, does not push,
and leaves the best places to women and children ; he
is never inquisitive or importunate and never tries to
teach people their business before he is asked ; he is
always courteous even to his subordinates and servants
and never forgets his 'please' and 'thank you' ;
he neither shouts nor uses abusive or rude language
any more than he is exaggeratedly amiable, but is courteous and correct and knows how to behave. 'What
can I do for you?' asks the English official of the
member of the public who comes to him about some
business or other ; it is only a form of words, of course,
but it is highly characteristic of the official's attitude to
the public. The Englishman's self-respect makes him
respect his neighbours, just as his love of freedom
makes him impose limitations on himself. The contacts
and relations with strangers incidental to daily life pass
off more pleasantly and with less friction in England
than anywhere else, because good manners are more
highly valued and bad manners more deeply looked down
on than elsewhere. Manners, it is said, are external,
but one's relations with everyone except one's closest
intimates are just as external, and of such is the greater
part of most people's lives made up. "Manners
Makyth Man" is the motto of one of the most ancient
Oxford Colleges, and a thoroughly English motto it is,

springing from the knowledge that the outward and the inward cannot be separated but stand in a reciprocal relation. Manners are fully as much bound up with character as, say, handwriting, gait or the lineaments of the face ; a man's character determines his exterior, but his exterior, conversely, has a formative effect on his character.

The Englishman is 'unnatural' in the sense that human beings as such are unnatural, since they are only distinguished from the beasts by certain repressions. A wild animal does no doubt live entirely 'according to nature' ; a domestic animal is already far from that, while a human being who followed his instincts to the full would in a very short time have to be rendered innocuous by his fellows. Civilization as it develops expresses itself in a constantly increasing number of more and more imperious inhibitions ; thus the Commandment "Thou shalt not kill" and the Commandment "Thou shalt not poke thy nose" only differ in degree of importance, not in essence. English customs and habits, commandments and prohibitions owe their triumph over so great a part of the globe to the fact that they testify to a very high stage in the evolutionary process that culminates in Man and do help this same evolution forward. There is no light without shade, of course ; civilized man cannot be a child of nature at the same time, nor can the fully-formed man of the world have the naivety of the primitive. But this is just where one of those peculiar features of the English character that make it so hard to understand comes in ; in spite of the Englishman's highly civilized manners, his strict conventions and his control over his feelings he emphatically does not live purely by the intellect ; on the contrary, he is, at the very bottom of his being, a non-rational mystic (possibly we are brought back to the prehistoric Celtic strain here) : the individual Englishman, and English policy too, often display a sureness of instinct almost as great as the sleep-walker's ; they often go along in one direction and then at some given moment start off in the opposite one ; they are absolutely illogical, but they get there. Everything in England is illogical, everything has something to counterbalance it and so avoid extremes, everything tends to correct itself, nothing leads to its logical conclusions. Logical consistency is confined to the intellectual, while a good half of the Englishman is non-rational. The English mind is neither a garden in which nature is subdued to geometry like the Latin mind, nor a primeval forest like the Slav mind, but a park where nature retains its rights so far as they are compatible with Man's convenience, a place that is neither natural nor artificial but a compromise between the two aims—in fact just like an English park.

Thus it is that the conventional Englishman is at the same time an enthusiastic lover of nature and a devotee of the simple life. He lives in the country if he possibly can, aims at simplicity and comfort in the arrangement of his house, wears sensible and easy clothes for every day, and finds company in the animal and vegetable creations. Instinctively reaching out after compensation for the voluntarily accepted repressions of civilization through close touch with what still belongs to nature, he carries nature into civilization and, conversely, civilization into nature ; for nothing is further from his thoughts than playing at being a peasant. The week-end in the country cottage, camping out in tents, and the caravan are just typically English inventions destined to make it possible to live in touch with nature without thereby relapsing into a 'state of nature.' There is also, however, undoubtedly a larger number of people in England than elsewhere who find the pressure of civilization intolerable and go out as pioneers to distant, primitive and as far as possible virgin lands. The whole of English colonial history is evidence of this, as it is equally of the fact that the Englishman takes English civilization so much as a matter of course, that it is so much part and parcel of his birthright, that the only thing he can possibly do anywhere, even in the wildest places, is to plant a little bit of England, with all the advantages and disadvantages of his native country.

The English attitude to life is a serious one. The country lies too far North to allow the care-free cheerfulness of the Neapolitan to flourish in it, but though the severity of the struggle for existence has made the Englishman tough, hard-working, reliable and conscientious, he does not enthuse over work and duty ; his heart is in play of some sort or other, whether in the way of sport or amusement. He does not save nor does he take much heed for the future : the Holiday Clubs of working people of both sexes, which are particularly numerous in Lancashire, the biggest industrial area, are a characteristic feature ; their members save up for the whole year, paying their contributions into a common fund, and then gleefully ' blow ' it in two or three days' holiday at one of the big seaside places, the favourite being Blackpool, which is a Luna Park on a vast scale. The working classes in particular are fond of amusement and allow themselves plenty of it, and most of it is extremely innocent ; for the English have a great deal of the child in their make-up. Thus their weapon against the seriousness of life is their sense of humour ; they are the great humorists among the nations and managed to make even the Great War yield its funny aspects. They are unrivalled in the development of their organs of ridicule, and nowhere does pomposity get so thoroughly laughed out of court and swollen head meet with such contempt as in England. Sense of humour means a sense of proportion in life ; the man who over-estimates his own importance is a comic figure, and to take one's joys and sorrows too seriously is to lack a sense of proportion. To this feeling of the ridiculousness of a lack of proportion add sympathy for the object of ridicule, based on the feeling that one is nearly as absurd oneself, and you have the peculiar English brand of humour. Nothing is more unbearable to the Englishman than emotionalism that does not ring true, theatricality and megalomania, but at the same time nothing is more alien to him than self-contempt or exaggerated meekness. Though he generally exaggerates neither his own importance nor other people's, he has a sound consciousness of his own position and lets his fellow-man have the same.

His manner of talking matches his character. His immense shyness of exaggerated expression inclines him rather to understatement. If he wants to say something really very nice about a friend he calls him 'rather a decent chap,' and when he cannot stand a man at any price he says he 'doesn't much care about' him. 'All right' and 'not bad,' whether applied to people, works of art or the beauties of nature, indicate a very high degree of approval. Of all words in the English of every-day life the most characteristic and the hardest worked is undoubtedly 'rather,' which tones down approval and censure equally. There are of course exceptions to this general way of talking : the East-Enders express themselves much more forcibly, and certain ultra-modern sets use highly emphatic (and quite meaningless) adjectives like 'absolutely divine' and 'perfectly devastating,' which correspond, incidentally, to the *fabelhaft* and *verheerend* of similar circles in Berlin. But they remain the exception, because emphatic expression makes an Englishman laugh.

The Englishman is, moreover, perhaps the only person in the world who can see the funny side of things and people without their falling in his estimation, the explanation being that, having a sense of humour, he starts with the conviction that they are not perfect. He does not treat the things he respects with anything like the deadly earnestness of other nations ; nowhere are public institutions such as the Police, the Civil Service or the Church so respected and even popular as in England, but that does not prevent their typical representatives—the Bobby with gigantic feet, the red-nosed old colonel, the timid stuttering curate and the pompous but henpecked vicar—from being standing figures of fun in the music-halls and comic papers. The Englishman is very much alive to the weaknesses of his countrymen and of the nation, but he forgives them and feels affection for them, and while the Parisian talks of his ' *Ville Lumière*,' the Londoner talks, with deep emotion, of ' dear, dirty old London.' A man like Edward VII was uncommonly popular just because of his well-known weaknesses—the pleasures of love and of the table ; while a man like Lord Curzon, because he was remote and had no vices, remained, in spite of the fullest recognition of his great merits, exceedingly unpopular.

English humour fits in remarkably well with English sentimentality, a mixture which one finds also in the Jewish character. Though the Englishman's sense of humour enables him to keep tragedy at arm's length, he likes a bit of an appeal to his feelings ; for the rest, he shares the inclination to sentimentality with most other nations, only in his case it is, perhaps, even stronger In English music-halls as in French *cafés chantants* the sentimental song is always the most successful one, and the American film, which represents the zenith of sentimentality, is first favourite all over the world. It is only the *gebildeten* that are ashamed of their sentimentality and disown it. The fear of being 'cheap' which prevails in the German intelligentsia is quite unknown in England, as it is, incidentally, in Latin countries too. Fear of 'cheap' sentiment is simply fear of giving way to the feelings in people who are not inwardly sure of themselves, while sentimentality is a symptom of health and unsophisticated simplicity. The sentimental film and the sentimental song or picture appeal to primitive unchanging emotions; compounded of Home, Mother, golden youth, first love, noble heroes, fair-haired Innocence, child-like ways, flower gardens, blue sky etc., they represent the world not as it is but as a childish dream would have it. It is all a bit blatant and crude and naive, but that is the only thing that distinguishes it from great poetry. Sentimentality is much nearer to great art than critical intelligence is, because both are matters of feeling originating in the unconscious. There is an immense difference of quality, but none of kind, between Shakespear's or Goethe's or Schiller's characters and those of popular sob-stuff; Schiller's Max and Thekla, Goethe's Gretchen and Klärchen, Shakespear's Ophelia and Juliet are of the same family as the characters acted by Mary Pickford and Lillian Gish; Lady Macbeth is the counterpart of the modern film Vamp, and Charlie Chaplin is the direct descendant of Shakespear's clowns. Sob-stuff for the most part only comes from want of tact in handling emotional material, a want of which the masses are not conscious.

The English have the same attitude to the productions of sentimental art as older children have to fairy tales;

they do not believe in them any longer, i.e. they know that they are not in the ordinary sense true, but they like listening to them because it would be lovely if they could be. The sentimentality of the Englishman is perfectly honest, like a child's, and thoroughly in harmony with his strong affection in real life for children, animals, gardens and flowers—for the idyllic, in fact; and it is only reasonable that it should gather greater strength the greater the contrast between his ideal and the actual surroundings of his daily life grows. The reason why sentimentality goes so well with a sense of humour is that they are both weapons of defence against the tragic side of life; the one enables man to escape for the moment into a world more in harmony with his dreams, the other takes the sting out of reality for him, and both spring from the instinct of self-preservation.

The Englishman has a tendency to ignore anything that might upset his natural optimism if he cannot alter it; as he does not want to have anything to do with it, he goes on as if it were not there, not speaking of it himself and not letting other people speak of it. This easily produces an effect of hypocrisy, and it is hypocrisy in a certain sense; yet it is also one side of the instinct of self-preservation. Thus it is impossible to get away from the fact that sex plays a very important part in human life, but the Englishman is determined that it shall not be publicly conspicuous; so one no more talks about it than one talks of digestion and other natural functions or devotes oneself to them in public. Since even the most savage races, as is well known, wear loin-cloths and surround their sexual ceremonies with mysteries, it is open to doubt whether the Anglo-Saxon attitude to sex represents a higher stage of civilization than that of other people or an unhealthy exaggeration. Judgement on the point is bound to be subjective; but it is certain that among other nations too, the higher and more civilized the class of the community you take, the more 'hypocritical' is its attitude to sex. The moral ideas of the peasant are very different from those of the patrician or aristocrat, for instance, and the difference is one of form; in just the same way the morals of the English are neither better nor worse than those of the French or the Germans but are stricter in form.

The English make no exhibition either of their vices or their virtues. One knows that sex exists and one knows in what varieties or vicious forms it finds expression in one's neighbour, just as one knows whether he is rich or in debt and whether his grandfather was a distinguished man of learning or a footpad; but it is not customary to make it a subject of conversation with him. Sex is a private affair in England. There are plenty of excrescences of Puritanism there, as everybody knows, and they are often grotesque enough; but when people quite rightly make fun of them, they ought to bear in mind the compensating fact that social intercourse between the sexes has for generations been infinitely freer and less constrained in England than in the majority of countries. The idea of comradeship between the sexes is a very old one in England; in France and Germany it is only beginning to be taken as a matter of course among the younger generation to-day. It is only possible where sex has ceased to be accepted as the one and only mainspring of existence and as an uncontrollable force of nature to which it is proper and necessary to yield, and where, on the contrary, self-control in these matters too is an unquestioned assumption. The fact is that a common system of education and the playing of games together have made great alterations in the relations of the sexes, and the entrance of women into innumerable professions which used to be the exclusive preserves of men has done the rest. That Woman's aureole of mystery has not suffered so terribly severely under these conditions is proved by the continued influence of the ideal of the Lady, which has already been discussed.

England is, further, the country in which the approximation of the ideals of masculine and feminine beauty to each other, which is now to be seen in all countries, first took place; in this matter also the English model has become supreme everywhere, and everywhere, consciously or unconsciously, people are striving to copy it. From England came the type of the slim cleanshaven athletic young man, to which even the old gentlemen there go on conforming. What has become of the lover with the *belle barbe*, or even the *moustache soyeuse* whom we meet in Maupassant, Bourget, and Marcel Prévost, or the typical young German officer or barrister, stiff and bristly-moustached? The young men in all countries, except in remote backward districts, all look exactly alike—like Englishmen, that is—and the women do not look very different. As late as the last generation the continental comic papers were full of the Englishwoman without bust or hips, who wore severe clothes hardly distinguishable from her husband's and walked with a firm step instead of tripping along; to-day Woman's World knows but one desire, to be slim. Hips and bust are got rid of as far as possible; *frou-frou*, frillies, wasp-waists, and in general all emphasis on femininity belong to the dim dark ages, and man and wife often look so alike as to be indistinguishable. That is the outward and visible sign that there has been a big change in the relation of the sexes to each other and a change in the Anglo-Saxon direction.

The freedom and equality for women which have

spread to the Continent from England are incompatible with the exaggerated cult of Woman as the ever-enticing and mysterious Eve, and reduce the importance of sex in reducing its mysteriousness. The greater the part played in life by sex, the smaller the freedom enjoyed by women ; to put it paradoxically, the greater Woman's power, the less her freedom, 'power' meaning power over Man's emotional life. At one end of the scale is the harem, at the other sex-equality, and the more a woman leads her own life the less is she the complement of the man. Thus in English literature, too, the man who comes to a bad end through love of a woman is as rare a figure as he was (but is no longer) common in French literature, and Byron's saying, "Man's love is of man's life a thing apart" is very typically English.

The fact that England is not the land of *crimes passionels* makes it the land of successful marriages. The institution of the *dot* is unknown there and people marry from inclination and not for advantage ; at the same time they seldom marry for passion either : in addition to love, professional and political considerations, friendship, and sport and games, which the man will not give up at any price, play their part. The man wants to preserve his liberty and keep up his interests even though he is married, and he lets his wife as far as possible do the same with hers : an English marriage implies a very high degree of mutual confidence. Moreover the Englishman is decidedly more domestic than the Continental : in England there are no regular *habitués*' tables in the beer-house and no *cafés*, nor does the Club count for much in the husband's life in the evening ; the average Englishman spends his evenings at home. On the other hand his wife is much less of a *Hausfrau* than her continental sister ; the children when they get older are educated at boarding schools much more commonly than on the Continent, so that, having more time to herself, she leads her own life to a greater extent. In this respect, too, husband and wife tend to approximate in their ways of going on, neither being pleasure-loving to excess. Though she has more time than he has, the frenzied pursuit of pleasure and sensation is alien to her too, apart from certain circles in Society. She is often quite a competent housewife but very seldom a keen one, and her interest in her kitchen and her linen-cupboard is kept within strict bounds. I quite believe that in England the poor man or the man in a small way does not find in his wife the unceasing economy, patience and industry that his French or German equivalent regards as a matter of course; his home is less well cared-for and his food is not so good, but his wife is less of a slave.

Drink and sport are the Englishman's big temptations, and the man who comes to a bad end through drink is a much more common phenomenon than the man whose life is wrecked by a *grande passion*. The tendency to drink is partly no doubt a matter of climate and race; it is also partly a relic of barbarism. Unlike the exhibition of other vices, being drunk is not socially regarded as a disgrace, and a tipsy man gets a kind of sympathy. In my belief that is simply a surviving relic of the mediaeval way of looking at things, a more or less isolated and unrelated bit of the John Bull ideal that will probably disappear before long—I refer not to drunkenness but to the sympathy for it. Drunkenness has been decreasing rapidly since the War, owing to legal regulations such as the lower percentage of alcohol in the drinks, and shorter hours. Here too the English seem to have found the sensible middle course between unrestricted freedom and Prohibition, with which the very pronounced decrease of crime in the country is certainly connected. In recent years there have been more murders recorded in the town of New York than in the whole of England, while London has less crime than any other great city, which is the most triumphant vindication that the ideal of Repression could have.

Sport, in every sense of the word, is an essential part of the Englishman's life. It includes betting, and cards are important too, though the real passion for gambling is not common enough to be described as a national characteristic; it is rather one side of his universal and very strongly marked 'play instinct,' which gives him a certain child-like or rather, youthful quality often into extreme old age, so that 'boyish' is, from him, the highest possible expression of respect and liking. The fact that the late Lord Balfour was in his seventies still a keen tennis player was a much greater title to fame than the fact that he had written important philosophical works. Intellectual things are as little in the average Englishman's line as they are in the average schoolboy's; they are alien, nay antipathetic, to him, even though they may possibly win his admiration. Setting much more store by human qualities than by intellectual ones, he likes a man who comes up to his idea of a 'good chap' much better than a clever man, and a really good chap with no instinct for games is for him quite inconceivable, in which he is perhaps not so far wrong. He brings the schoolboy's ideals of fair play, sportsmanship, and 'cricket' into every walk of life—business, politics and human relations; and when, as in questions of foreign and colonial policy, he keeps them absolutely out of the picture, which English policy does do to at least as great an extent as any other country's, the political leaders and their henchmen among the Press strain every nerve to cover up the fact and twist it round till the multitude is convinced of the disinterestedness of the motive which is swaying the Government. Thus the English keep hold of India because otherwise the Mohammedans would fall upon the Hindus, and they took part in the War to defend Little Belgium. They are all righteousness and compassion; unfortunately the enemy of the moment is a devil in human shape whom it is impossible to encounter on fair terms as one can an Englishman. Naturally the people are as easily convinced of this as they are in other countries. It is a mistake to accuse the whole nation of hypocrisy; it believes the stories it is told quite honestly, because everyone readily believes what suits him. This hypocrisy, which is a part of the British technique of government, is, they say, 'a compliment that vice pays to virtue.' I do not believe that politics have ever been conducted in any country or at any period without hypocrisy; still, this technique has nowhere reached so high a pitch of perfection as in England, perhaps because the people who invent the lies unconsciously believe they are true and hope that things really are as they would be, should be and could not help being in a world guided by an all-British Providence.

V

TOWN AND COUNTRY

An English town is no more the same thing as a continental town than the English country is equivalent to what is called the country on the Continent. 'Town' for the Englishman strictly speaking means only one place, London, and living anywhere else is living 'in the country,' London being a thing apart. This usage does not, I need hardly say, prevent the existence of innumerable towns both great and small apart from London; England can, in fact, boast of forty towns of more than 100,000 inhabitants; it may, however, have arisen from the realization that the metropolis is the only real city, none of the other big towns of England being much more than centres of trade, industry or shipping, business centres surrounded by residential villages. The word 'province' in its continental sense is unknown in England, nor is there any reality to which it would correspond; for a 'province' implies a special character of its own, in a way that is unknown in England. Munich differs from Hamburg, Marseilles from Lille, in customs and appearance, but the big towns of England, apart from peculiarities of situation, are all alike. The residential quarters of Newcastle look exactly like those of Plymouth, and a business thoroughfare in Birmingham exactly like one in Nottingham or Bradford.

Apart from a few old buildings, the big towns are characterized by a dreary monotony, and the industrial centres among them by extreme hideousness ; they are just a business quarter plus suburbs, utilitarian and unbeautiful. There are no former capitals in England, and you hardly ever find a palace in the big towns ; true, they are in many cases of very ancient origin, but they have never been centres of court or aristocratic civilization ; they owe their existence to the middle classes and their expansion to the proletariat. No one lives in them from inclination or taste, as one might live in Dresden or Munich or Florence or Geneva ; people either earn their livings in them or stay on in them because they were born there. Creations of the trading middle classes, they nearly all bear the stamp of the nineteenth century ; their creators built their houses of business and round the business centre so formed, for which they had no feeling, they erected their comfortable small detached houses—rows of low-built villas, each with its little garden, covering the country round for miles. The working-class quarters are more crowded, more squalid, with even less character about them, but otherwise the same. In the older towns you may find a fine old church here and there and perhaps a Guildhall ; the biggest of them boast a museum in the Classical style, or university buildings, and a theatre or a music-hall, and that is all. They are towns with no legends attaching to them, haunted by no ghosts, informed by no spirit, the dwelling-place of mediocrity, of the average respectable man, with no soul in them, soul not being a useful commodity. They have, of course, the qualities of their defects—that is, they are comfortable ; an inhabitant of Bradford or Bristol enjoys very much better housing conditions than his colleague in the same walk of life in Roubaix or Genoa. The standard of living of the middle classes is much higher in England, with houses, clothes and servants all of a higher grade, and the same is true of the artisan ; on the other hand the 'submerged tenth' is even worse off in those respects, and larger in numbers, than in other countries. The streets are well looked-after and well lighted, there are well-kept parks and gardens everywhere, and schools, hospitals etc. are thoroughly first-rate. It is a well-arranged utilitarian middle-class world, from which art, imagination and the things of the Spirit have been almost completely eliminated.

These towns are not comparable with towns of long-established *bourgeois* culture like the German Hansa Towns or Free Cities, for instance, and the Dutch, Flemish or Italian towns. Augsburg, Nüremberg and Lübeck, Bruges and Amsterdam, Venice, Genoa, Pisa and Florence were states with a political life and a civilization, brought into being by rich and artistic merchant princes ; each was an enclosed world in itself, and so were the petty capitals too in their way. The English merchants who in the nineteenth century determined the character of Manchester and Liverpool, Birmingham, Leeds and Sheffield, knew no ambition beyond the comfortable residential and industrial town ; where a town does display interest in something not material, as Manchester, for example, does in music, the phenomenon causes great surprise. Isolated cases of old traditions notwithstanding, the big towns of England are really no more than colonial towns, without individuality and without charm. One has to consider the way they grew up. Ever since the twelfth century England has known only one metropolis : the whole process of development extending from the Middle Ages to modern times, which on the Continent produced, after the fortified towns of feudalism, the cities of the Renaissance merchant princes and the capitals of the eighteenth century, had no influence on the English towns, which remained small and obscure till the prodigious growth of industry and trade in the nineteenth century drove hordes of people into them, who hastily put up places to live and work in. It is these facts, and not some inferiority in their inhabitants, that are responsible for their unrelieved drabness; where the same causes were at work on the Continent they produced the same effects, and Essen and Barmen, Verviers and Tourcoing are fully as dreary as any town in England.

The small towns are a very different story. Unlike the Continent, where the small town is a reproduction in miniature of the bigger town, as the bigger town is of the great city, so that you can infer from the number of their inhabitants what attractions they have to offer, the big cities of England are without exception industrial centres of the type described above, while the medium-sized and small towns are of a quite different character and, so far as they are not merely commercial centres on a small scale, quite unlike anything else.

First there are the cathedral towns, which are among the greatest attractions of the country. Its magnificent cathedrals, dating from the Norman and Gothic periods, are most of them in small country towns, having grown out of abbeys; only in rare cases were they built by wealthy citizens to be the glory of some great city. It is the cathedral that takes first place, the town exists but to minister to it. These vast buildings do not raise their towering heads from a mass of mean narrow streets; they lie stretched out on green lawns, shaded by immemorial trees, each in its close, round which the houses of the clergy are grouped and, in many cases, a wall still runs. The Cathedral and its satellite buildings—the chapter-house, the bishop's palace, the schools and almshouses—form the real town, the rest being a mere adjunct, and the way this town blends with the landscape, both together forming a single whole, is an achievement of landscape-architecture truly symbolical of England. For it is only where he finds himself in contact with nature that the Englishman produces great architecture like his cathedrals, country houses and monasteries : the idea of the town as a work of art is alien to him ; he has, in sharp contrast to the Latin, no affection for it, and never ceases to regard it as something forced upon him, an unpleasant necessity from which he seeks to escape. Instead of planning his towns, he lets them grow anyhow and introduces some sort of order as an after-thought ; even their main streets are old country roads, following the lie of the country in their winding course, and their lay-out has been determined not by thought but by the hazard of nature. This tendency, which is a weakness where town-planning is concerned, is extremely valuable when it comes to inserting single buildings or group of buildings into the landscape ; then it produces unique combinations of art and nature such as the cathedral and castle of Durham on their hill, the cathedral and college buildings of Winchester, and *ensembles* like those of York, Canterbury, Ely and so many other places, where walls and towers, spires and roofs, trees, gardens, hills and meadows unite to form a composition of an indescribable charm, which comes from the blending of magnificent architecture with the peaceful rural landscape.

These cathedral towns are not dead, because Christianity is still a living thing in England ; they are alive, but with the life of another age, knowing nothing of unrest and hurry and the scramble for money and pleasure, with a horizon which, though narrow, is complete in itself. Canterbury is quite as truly English as

Birmingham is, and to grasp that fact is the beginning of understanding England. England gets her living from the Birminghams, but the Canterburies have her heart, and when, as sometimes happens, Time turns a Canterbury into a Birmingham, the Englishman laments the change instead of regarding it as progress.

Akin to the cathedral towns are the two university towns of Oxford and Cambridge, which, springing entirely from ecclesiastical foundations, have followed a line of development peculiar to themselves, to the description of which a later chapter of this book is devoted.

Another important type of English town is the county town, which has disappeared from the industrial areas but everywhere else remains a little centre for the country round and the market-town of its district. Its life is agricultural and its population consists of squires, tenant-farmers and villa-dwellers, the peasant being a thing of the past. The county towns remind one of Dickens, as the cathedral towns do of the Middle Ages; though many of them can boast an ancient castle, like Warwick, or an ancient church, their really characteristic feature is the comfortable old inns, where the coaches used to stop. There is not much of them beyond the irregular straggling High Street, which is simply a bit of the main road, and a regular square or open space is a rarity in these little Saxon towns. It is surprising, especially to the foreigner, how good the shops are; the explanation is that here are the tailor, the shoemaker and the coach-builder (and in these days the branches of the motor-car makers) who work for the country houses, big provision shops too, and, in many cases, branches of London firms. A town like Guildford, with its contented and well-to-do air, seems like a bit of 'merrie England' that has stood still since 1830— a pleasant half-way house between town and country for elderly people not too well blessed with this world's goods, and such people do in fact tend to choose the neighbourhood of towns of this sort to settle in. It remains to say that the cathedral town and the county town are often one and the same place, exhibiting a blend of the characteristics of both.

Certain towns are completely given over to retired Colonial Civil Servants and soldiers and people living on their investments: most of them are spas supposed to be particularly healthy, e.g. Leamington, Harrogate, Cheltenham, and, most charming of them all, Bath, the favourite resort of the gay and careless world of fashion in the eighteenth century, which has preserved the spirit of that period in its lay-out and its architecture, though Society has long since deserted it and in fact now only goes to foreign spas and watering-places like Deauville, Biarritz, Cairo and the Lido. To the same category belong many of the seaside towns which have long ceased to be mere watering-places and have become residential towns and, in some cases like Brighton and Bournemouth, very large towns and distant suburbs of London. A number of country towns can be traced back to Roman sites; these are mostly distinguished by the termination -cester (=*castrum*) and have their two straight main streets crossing at right-angles; often a church stands on the site of an ancient temple, and in some cases, Chester for example, Renaissance houses and Gothic cathedrals have been fitted into the Roman ground-plan. Here and there one finds a sleepy little town dreaming of its past, like Rye or Winchelsea, which were once big ports but are now far inland. The country towns of England are as charming and full of variety as the big towns are dreary and monotonous, and the point is that they are *country* towns—that is, in the manner of life, views and tastes of their inhabitants, in fact in their whole nature, they do not come into the category of 'town' at all, but are part of the country.

'The Country' in the English sense, with all the associations that the word carries, is peculiar to England. The Frenchman's or German's 'country' is intersected by straight roads and covered with plough-land or potato-fields or maybe vineyards; its villages are inhabited by peasants and stalled cattle; the townsman is a strange and ridiculous phenomenon there, fundamentally different from the dweller in the country in the clothes he wears, the way he lives and in his attitude to things in general; for the two live in different periods altogether. Or if it is not that it is 'scenery,' with a conscious appeal to the sightseer, like the Hartz Mountains or the Vosges, the Lake of Geneva or the Rhine, full of hotels, visitors and views. England has very little tourist country of that sort—only the Lake District, the Highlands, parts of Wales and certain bits of the coast; but there is 'country' everywhere the moment one gets away from the town.

Without either the pretensions of 'magnificent scenery' or the uninspiringness of continental 'country,' the English countryside resembles neither a famous Beauty nor a peasant woman. There being very little agriculture, it is mostly pastoral, with stretches of green meadowland, of that deep green that one only gets in this damp insular climate, swelling into little hills and criss-crossed like a chess-board with green hedges between the fields, while the roads wind along like snakes between the tall green hedgerows and the footpaths cut across the green grass—you seldom walk along a dusty road in England, you cut across the fields and through the hedges. Everywhere you see scattered groups of trees, each tree a most orderly, isolated individual developing freely on its own lines. You will not find many forests—forests belong to a more primitive stage of development—and no rows of trees along the roads—that would be too thought-out ; what you do find is single trees, each living its own life as a good Englishman should, and cattle, horses and sheep grazing everywhere in apparent freedom. It is Arcadia. The country is in fact a vast park, disfigured here and there by blots in the shape of urban and industrial areas, and with separate smaller and still better-kept parks inside it ; in its present-day aspect it is a work of art created in the inspiration of definite ideals, and the impression it gives of existing for the pleasure of mankind apart from any utilitarian aim, precisely as a work of art does, is very near the truth.

The country is a creation of the English aristocracy, and the people of England are in a certain sense the aristocracy of the British Empire, able to allow themselves the luxury of this park. The Norman barons built their strongholds on the land granted to them ; later generations converted them into castles and palaces ; in the Renaissance or Baroque periods gardens and parks were laid out round them, and the land ministered to the large landowners' pleasures—hunting and shooting, riding, fishing and games. The free peasants were turned into dependent tenant farmers, and agriculture progressively disappeared as England became a centre of international trade, and corn, vegetables, fruit, meat and butter came in from foreign countries and the Colonies, which also provided her industries with their raw materials. Relieved from the necessity of work, the country was in a position to be beautiful and beautiful it became : that is how it came to be the Englishman's ideal to live in the country. The aristocracy that has been the ruling class since Norman times (with the exception of the short period of the Puritan revolution) was wise enough constantly to absorb new elements and not stand out for exclusiveness, thanks to which policy it survived every change that time brought and, instead of bringing the hatred of the populace on itself as the continental aristocracies did, became—and remained—its ideal. The life of a country gentleman is what every Englishman dreams of and consciously or unconsciously takes as his model.

The English country gentleman, his house and the way he lives constitute, at their best, the highest achievement of English civilization, the finest flower of aristocratic culture certainly, perhaps of the whole culture of the white races. In order that the minority may have such a good time, the majority has to have a distinctly less good one, and the aristocracy is the privileged minority of the English people, as the English nation is among the subjects of the British Empire. The Englishman, with his governing-class ideal, is an unconscious Nietzschean but leaves open to everybody the possibility, and consequently the hope, of rising to that privileged class. The significant fact is not merely that new titles are conferred in large quantities—titles are not really very important in England—but that new blood is constantly being introduced into country life. The rich tradesman or industrialist, having bought or built himself a country house, sooner or later gets into 'county' society, i.e. becomes one of the ruling class, which carries with it the local seat in Parliament and other such things; conversely the nobility have long since taken to engaging directly or indirectly in commerce and industry. Distinctions are disappearing and the ruling class has very much broadened its basis in the nineteenth and twentieth centuries, so that the 'country' retains its importance, without producing an

antithesis between itself and town ; and it is naturally
losing some of its character in the process. The real
country gentlemen, sportsmen and friends of art and
culture, who built those lovely old country houses with
their art treasures, libraries and collections and took a
personal interest in all the inhabitants of their locality,
the kind that did in fact justify the admiration accorded
to the type, are getting fewer every day and disappearing
in the multitude of those who have not got, or have not
yet acquired, those traditions, and whose connexion
with the country and its people is quite on the surface.
The tradition, however, is at present still so strong
that the new-comers gradually grow into it.

The population of the country does not consist
exclusively of owners of great houses ; it includes
untold masses of middle-class folk, who build their
houses, with big gardens, parks and meadows, close to
the towns or villages, many of the latter being entirely
inhabited in these days by people of this type. Living
there is cheaper and healthier than in the town, which
in a country so densely populated as England is never
far off, so that it is possible to enjoy its attractions
without living in it. From the real town house by
way of the surburban villa with its garden to these houses
in the country it is only a series of gradations, and there is
no sharp contrast dividing urban and country life, but
anyone who can gravitates towards the country : he is
faced with no competing urban ideal; for the Englishman's ambition is not to live in the metropolis as the
Frenchman's is to live in Paris, but to live in the country,
and the better off he is, the more completely he realizes
this ideal, which is for ever beyond the reach of the poor.
The magnificent country houses and the terrible slums
of the big towns form a contrast in which the two sides,
both unparalleled on the Continent, are reciprocally

connected ; for, if the population of the country had not been swallowed up by the industrial towns and there were still a numerous free peasantry, the country would be less of a Garden of Eden, the towns less dreary.

Whether the attempt to reduce the large estates by legislation and high death duties and create a body of small-holders will succeed remains to be seen. In itself it follows the traditional trend of English policy towards extending the privileges of the upper classes to increasingly wide sections of the population and thus avoiding violent struggles ; on the other hand, as has been shown, agriculture is impossible in England without protective tariffs, which would send up the cost of living. Besides, it looks as if the desire of the English proletariat to live in the country, which does not mean at all the same thing to it as it does to the upper classes, were not a strong one ; in spite of all the disadvantages they prefer the town with its pleasures and its gregariousness and get bored in the country. It is my belief that the artificial re-settlement of the land will break down ; for one thing, the future is with the industrial garden-city, and further, we may take it that modern inventions and continual improvements in the means of transport will rapidly alter the character of the country, particularly as distances in England are anyhow so small. It will very soon be possible to live in the country and work in town, and the twentieth century will make the contrast between them less sharp and perhaps eliminate it. Here, too, England is going her own way.

Nearly all English poetry is connected with nature and scenery. The country is England's poetry, the town her prose, which is just the reverse of the position in Latin countries—one has but to think of the towns of Italy, for instance. From the English point of view, town represents constraint, nature freedom, and it is likely that as England's country gets more and more towny, an increasing number of her sons will be driven by the craving for more unspoiled nature, greater solitude and freedom to leave their mother country and go to the Dominions. It is my opinion that such an old and firmly established ideal as the English one cannot be changed, but will come to the surface again even in the urban proletariat, the more so as the industrial development of England has undoubtedly passed its zenith. The Englishman wants to be his own master, he wants his own house on his own land where no one shall say him nay—in a word, independence : his ambition is to be a country gentleman. England is the land of the great stock-breeder and the individual prize specimen ; in the same way as it breeds unsurpassed race-horses, dogs, prize cattle, roses, orchids and peaches, it has also bred a human type, the individual developed at the expense of the masses ; but being also the land of wisdom and strong humane feeling, it tries to soften and cover up excessively sharp contrasts and raise the largest possible numbers of the race to a higher level. To-day, when the growth of the vast urban proletariat has made the contrasts undoubtedly greater than ever before, the task is a prodigiously hard one ; but there is no doubt that even the English radical does not, at the bottom of his heart, aim at a process of levelling down He does not want to destroy aristocracy ; he would like to be an aristocrat himself, and would, if he had the power, turn England not into a town but into a homestead of free people living as seems them good. English ideals for the future lie far more in the direction of anarchism than of communism.

VI

LONDON

London resembles no other place in the world ; it is unlike any English town, even more unlike any town outside England. It is not a town at all, but a formation for which no name exists : nobody can state definitely where London begins or ends, how far it extends or how many inhabitants it musters ; the County of London created in the nineteenth century has four and a half millions, the Metropolitan Police area seven and a half, the proposed London Health District something like ten millions. All these are purely administrative divisions ; London in its entirety is beyond measurement, only the City, its historical core, having boundaries.

Roman and mediaeval London was a city like other European cities, surrounded by walls within which stood the public buildings, churches and dwellings of the citizens. The City has preserved innumerable old customs and even to-day remains a separate entity with its own government and its own police. In a sense it is London ' proper,' but this London Proper musters not more than 13,000 inhabitants, a population of doorkeepers. It is exclusively a business centre, and that only in a certain restricted sense ; it consists, that is, of banks, offices of shipping and insurance companies etc., but both the big emporiums and stores and pretty well everything connected with the Port of London, the biggest port in the world, lie outside it. It is a gigantic office seething with millions of people and vast business by day, completely dead at night and on Sundays.

The City is the centre of London's gigantic structure but only its business centre ; as such, however, it bears absolutely no resemblance to the deliberately planned business centre of an American or other modern town. Every inch of the City is historic ground where every period has left its traces : its centre is Royal Exchange Place on which the Royal Exchange, the Bank of England and the Mansion House, which is the residence of the Lord Mayor, abut. The architecture of these buildings bears the stamp of the eighteenth and early nineteenth centuries (not of the present age), but the places where they stand to-day were already occupied by the buildings of the Roman Forum. The streets are all narrow, winding and mediaeval in character, bear historical and sacred names derived from remote antiquity and are intersected by many courts and passages. The City contains innumerable churches, the largest and most magnificent being St. Paul's Cathedral, the gigantic dome of which dominates it ; most of them were rebuilt in the seventeenth century after the Great Fire which destroyed half London, but some of the most ancient of them, dating from the Norman and Gothic periods, escaped destruction, as did the Gothic Guildhall, whereas most of the Halls of the still-existent Guilds are modern buildings. The nineteenth and twentieth centuries have come and built their palatial banks and offices in these narrow alleys ; but here and there old houses, even half-timbered ones, still stand, and one comes up against a church at every second step. The City is in plan a mediaeval town, like Sienna or Lübeck ; its buildings are mostly modern commercial buildings, among which numerous survivals of past centuries, chiefly ecclesiastical, raise their heads. Below, the block of office buildings crowded together ; up in the sky the white of innumerable towers (it is a peculiarity of London that the upper part of the buildings retain the original white of the stone) ; soaring above them all, the dome of St. Paul's—these form a picture the like of which no other town can show.

A closer examination of the City—in area a very small place—reveals the fact that even this tiny little bit of London is not so easy to define ; for it is not exclusively a business centre. Certain trades and professions are still concentrated, in true mediaeval fashion, in their own special quarters, some of which are within its boundaries. The way into the City from the West takes you to the site of its old gate, Temple Bar. Once the property of the Knights Templars, the Temple has belonged since the Reformation to the lawyers, who have also in the course of time occupied the whole of the surrounding quarter. On the left the first building inside the City that you see is the vast neo-Gothic Law Courts ; on the right are gateways leading to the Temple, one of the most peculiar and characteristic places in London. In it are situated the ancient church containing the tombs of the Templars, two Great Halls, in one of which Shakespear gave gala performances, and the garden in which he (incorrectly) sets the beginning of the Wars of the Roses, as well as numerous courts and buildings, mostly dating from the eighteenth century and occupied almost exclusively by lawyers. There are several other institutions similar to the Temple dating from the Renaissance, such as Lincoln's Inn, Gray's Inn and the rest—also enclosed groups of buildings with chapels, halls, libraries, gardens, courts and chambers. All these together are known as the Inns of Court and, as they are all close to each other, they make this whole bit of the City a unique thing, a town of lawyers in an architectural setting of the greatest charm, where the monasteries of the Law form islands of quiet and beauty in the sea of business.

The Inns of Court are the High Place of English jurisprudence ; to qualify as a barrister it is necessary to have read for a certain number of terms there and to have consumed in their halls a certain number of dinners, by which according to immemorial custom a student's seniority is reckoned, each term containing such and such a number of dinners ; so if you ask a young man what his profession is you may get the answer that he is 'eating his dinners,' which is puzzling to the foreigner but means that he is reading for the Bar.

The main traffic street in this western end of the City is Fleet Street, the headquarters of British journalism, where the offices of all the London newspapers and many provincial and colonial ones, and of the reviews, magazines and illustrated papers, are all crowded together. Thus do the Law and Journalism both have their share of dominion over the City, which can boast two further oases in the Charterhouse and the bit of green round St. Paul's, besides views over the river, across which London Bridge has from time immemorial and through all its endless transformations formed the entrance to it.

The City, the West End and the East End are the parts of London of which everybody knows and, were there no more to it, it would be a standard great city, with its centre, its rich residential quarter in the West, and its poor one in the East. But these make up only a small part of London. The West End, far from being homogeneous, is an extremely complicated structure, the different quarters of which display absolutely distinct characters. The part that lies nearest to the

City is the tourist centre, where the theatres and restaurants are, and is what the majority of foreigners mean by 'London' without further qualification. It has a greater resemblance than any other part of this gigantic place to a continental capital, and, as far as its main streets and squares go, less character, to say the least of it. Here, crowded into quite a small area, are forty to fifty theatres and music-halls, innumerable cinemas, huge modern hotels, big blocks of offices and buildings of the Dominions. Then there is the Strand, resort of overseas visitors ; Trafalgar Square and the National Gallery ; the Embankment ; Leicester Square, the centre of London's 'boulevard' life ; and Piccadilly Circus, London's equivalent of the Place de l'Opéra or the Potsdamer Platz. This part of the town is only beautiful by night, when the sky signs transform it into a fantastic spectacle and the evening dresses, jewels and motor cars of the theatre and restaurant public bring wealth and luxury into its drab streets.

The part that lies a little further to the West, containing Regent Street, Bond Street etc., is just the opposite ; its beauty is an affair of daylight. It is the shopping town, where the big stores, the smart little shops and the old-established specialist firms are, and the home of the jewellers, dressmakers and art-dealers. A special feature of London is its innumerable men's luxury shops ; London is the head-quarters of men's fashions for the whole world, and there are certain streets occupied almost entirely by men's tailors.

At this point the town begins once more to exhibit a quite peculiar character, in the region of St. James's. Pall Mall, street of palatial clubs, is unthinkable anywhere but in London ; so is St. James's Street where, in the window of the most famous hat maker in the world, which has remained as it was since the eighteenth century, you can look at the hats of the great ones of that period, while a vast canary-yellow coach stands side by side with the motor cars in a coach-builder's. St. James's is the region of fashionable young men, from Byron to the Prince of Wales who resides, appropriately, in St. James's Palace. Round St. James's Park, however, lies the London that is the capital of the greatest Empire in the world, and from a little bridge over the lake in the park you can, with a slight stretch of the imagination, survey the British Empire and the history of England. There is Buckingham Palace, the residence of the King, with the great Queen Victoria's Memorial, only bearable at a distance, standing in front of it, and the residences of other members of the Royal Family, Embassies and Palaces nearby. Over there are Nelson's Column and the Duke of York's Column, and the palatial government offices of Whitehall, shuffled and piled one above the other by the tricks of perspective—the Admiralty, the Colonial Office, the Home Office, the India Office, the Foreign Office—and the little old house in Downing Street where the Prime Minister lives, a figure of possibly greater significance than his opposite number in the Palace. You can see the Banqueting Hall of Charles I, in front of which he was beheaded—that spot and that day mark the beginning of the French Revolution and of the Bolshevik one too—and over there the Gothic towers, old and new, of Westminster, the heart of the British Empire, stretch up to Heaven. In that splendid Gothic Abbey sleep England's kings and her great men, and Elizabeth and Mary Stuart, Shakespear and the Unknown Soldier are near neighbours. Here on an ancient Gothic throne, England's highly constitutional monarchs are crowned amid mediaeval ceremonial ; next door is Westminster Hall, the oldest parliament house in the world, in which a divinely anointed king was for the first time condemned to death by his subjects ; behind are the gigantic modern Houses of Parliament. Here are the living symbols of English tradition and English revolution, that inseparable pair whose mingling can alone make England intelligible.

The London of Westminster is the proudest capital in the world, the symbol in stone of the greatest empire in history. St. James's Park begins the chain of lovely parks round which lie the aristocratic and wealthy districts of Mayfair and Belgravia and, further out, Kensington and Chelsea, which correspond to the West End of Berlin or the Champs-Elysées district of Paris but are totally unlike them. Rich or in narrow circumstances, the Englishman wants a house of his own— only here and there does a block of flats raise its solitary bulk to the sky—and the lay-out of the place is quite different. The present residential districts of London were all once separate places, and each has one or two streets that are entirely commercial while the rest of it consists entirely of residential streets and squares : consequently life in London is far quieter and far less urban, with a quiet street and only a few people living in the house, which often has a garden. Everything is well kept, shut off and exclusive, and each district, almost each street, is occupied by people of one class, so that a Londoner's address gives away his social position. Mayfair and Belgravia are the preserve of the aristocracy, who have their palatial town houses here, diversified by American, colonial, Jewish and native millionaires ; the houses are large and mostly Classical in style, dating from the eighteenth or the early nineteenth century, and their plain exteriors, which depend only on good proportions for their effect, give no hint of the masses of art treasures they contain.

Kensington is the district of the rich *bourgeoisie* outside Society, and its houses are newer and bigger but strike one as less distinguished—as Victorian in fact. Its museums, the vast Victoria and Albert Museum of fine and applied art, the Indian Collections, the Natural History Museum and the Imperial College of Science and Technology form a regular town of their own. The word 'Kensington' conveys a slight touch of over-fed middle-class philistinism; Kensington is wealthy, but it is not smart. The neighbouring district of Chelsea is very different, being a mixture of artists' quarter and fashionable streets and squares. It was the home of Carlyle, Rossetti and Whistler, whose studies of fog were made by the river here. Its houses, shops and restaurants all have an arty air about them, the very self-consciousness of which has, incidentally, rather got on the nerves of the younger generation of artists and caused them to migrate to districts not yet stamped as 'artistic.'

It is impossible to enumerate all the parts of London and give their characteristics; all one can do is to pick one out here and there, and for the rest make the general remark that they are all part of the picture which is London. There is Soho, the French and Italian quarter, with its innumerable cheap dressmakers and little restaurants, a somewhat doubtful plantation of exotics hidden away in the district of the hotels and theatres. There is Bloomsbury, district of big squares enclosed by beautiful harmoniously proportioned eighteenth-century houses, once an aristocratic quarter, now full of private hotels, the patrons of which draw one's attention to the fact that the heart of Bloomsbury is the British Museum. Here, full of book shops and antique shops, is the London of the learned from every country and the cheap but knowledge-craving American tourists. Hampstead, high on its hill, is prosperous and has artistic and cultural ambitions ; its modern villas might be in Grunewald. Bayswater is the district of cheap shops and cheap boarding-houses.

All these contiguous districts are only a part of the Greater West End. East of the City and South of the river stretch huge monotonous working-class districts, with great main streets miles long and full of noisy traffic and for the rest nothing but a maze of little mean streets of squalid little brick houses, from which here and there a church or a public-house stands out. There are the manufacturing districts, and Woolwich, the Chinese Quarter and Whitechapel, the Eastern Jews' Ghetto, with its markets, its Yiddish theatre, its Ring and its own university college. South of the river there are the lovely Baroque Greenwich Hospital and Greenwich Park, which come as a surprise in this poverty-stricken neighbourhood, and docks, granaries and warehouses everywhere along the river, forming the greatest port in the world, which is cut up into little sections and hidden away, a mere name to most Londoners. Interminable poor and lower-middle class districts spread away to North and South over flat ground and hills, and more flat ground and more hills, countless, mysterious places, of which only their inhabitants have any conception, while to the rest of the world they are mere names. Not till we have passed them do we come to the wide belt of the suburbs. Kew, Richmond and Hampton Court are to London what Potsdam is to Berlin and Versailles to Paris ; only the town has long ago reached them and swallowed them up, sending out to them underground railways, motor buses and long rows of houses. First comes a belt of older suburbs with the forbidding stucco houses of the Victorian age ; then, less closely packed, the white walls and red roofs of the twentieth century, golf-courses and play-grounds, commons, an occasional bit of meadow-land, and then again new settlements with rows of houses and streets of shops—hundreds of little towns and all bits of London—till finally there comes the last solitary row of houses followed by nothing but rural peace, and we are in the country.

A mosaic that never forms a whole, made up of the City, the West End and the East End, of lots of little towns and innumerable suburbs—that is what London is. The metropolis of a people that has no love for towns, a shapeless mass dumped down as circumstances dictated according to the lie of the country, the biggest port and biggest business centre in existence, a gigantic pleasure resort, the city of the rich and of the poorest of the poor, the home of all nations, full of unspeakable monotony and of unbelievable variety, absolutely modern, absolutely mediaeval, absolutely eighteenth-century or absolutely middle-class-Victorian, according to the point of view one takes up. It is safe to say anything about it, for anything will hit the mark ; thus it is at once the proudest of imperial cities and a Saxon village ; the rendezvous of the scum of the earth and the home of the most highly-bred aristocracy in the world ; a Hell, a Paradise and an interminable grey Purgatory. Nobody knows or can know London really thoroughly : for it means something different to everybody. To the working classes it signifies a dark interminable desert of brick, with gin-palaces and cinemas for oases ; to the man of the lower-middle class, a little house with a garden surrounded by other houses just like it, from which the Underground takes him to the City ; to the well-to-do man, the respectable district in which numerous other well-to-do people, as respectable as himself, live, plus a little business, something in the way of games, Church on Sundays and an occasional visit to the theatres, restaurants and shops of the West End ; to the world of the Great, the seat of the Court and the place where, according to immemorial usage, they spend the Season, and the period of Court functions, dances, race-meetings, athletic events, first nights and exhibitions—in short, of an indefatigable pursuit of pleasure lasting several months ; to the Member of Parliament, the politician, the lawyer and the financier, the spot from which the world is governed.

London is not a city but a hundred cities, not a whole but a thousand parts, at once more towny and more countrified than any other capital in the world, more impressive and less grand, a haphazard production guided by practical sense, as metropolitan as they are made and as provincial too. It has something of everything in it—the English provincial town, the university town, the county town, the continental capital, the sea-port town, the American business centre, the mediaeval Hansa town, the Baroque capital—and yet it is like nothing but itself. It is at once a chaos and a world ; the capital city of a race of Saxon peasants, a mediaeval Chivalry, a Hanseatic merchant community, an industrial country, a race of traders and sailors, a gigantic proletariat, an almost equally large lower-middle class, a rich upper-middle class and a brilliant Society ; the metropolis of England, Great Britain and the British Empire, that is, to-day, of a quarter of the human race.

London's exterior cannot be considered apart from the character, customs and habits of its population. England is a land of individualists, in which each class, each profession, each district, each house keeps itself to itself. Where, as in the newer suburbs, houses are built in rows or blocks for the sake of economy, every house must at least have its own name or be distinguished from its neighbours by different paint or a different sort of fence. The mansion flat, in spite of its many advantages, has not achieved popularity in London, which remains the city of innumerable small or tiny houses.

The Englishman sets infinite store by his house, far more than the inhabitants of other big cities usually do by their habitations, and as regards housing he is in many ways a spoilt child of fortune. By a payment of £50 down even the small man can acquire a house of his own, price £750–£1,000. The typical upper-middle class house is comfortable and roomy; it goes without saying that it contains a day-nursery for the children, and the servants' quarters are good, including a sitting-room for them (more than one in the bigger houses), which nobody on the Continent appears to consider necessary. These houses are sensibly and comfortably appointed. I am not saying that every sitting-room in England is a masterpiece of interior decoration, but at least bad taste is rare, as the English like things simple and unpretentious. Their bedrooms are bedrooms and nothing else, simple and hygienic; their drawing-rooms are not reception-rooms but living-rooms; their dining-rooms are the right size to hold the family and a few friends, not vast chambers in which they give dinner parties: to make up for that, even small houses nearly always have a spare room, and large ones a number of them; for the Englishman is extremely hospitable to his friends and entertains extensively.

In no other town is it so important, nay essential, to have good friends, because practically everything that constitutes the charm of London life takes place behind closed doors, either of clubs or private houses; nowhere does street-life count for so little. The Englishman is averse from exhibiting himself in public and still more so from mixing with a crowd of strangers. The function of the London street is simply to contain the traffic, which is so dense that its stream sweeps the individual along with it. To go for a stroll in the street is almost impossible ; it is all one can do to stop in front of a shop window : for walking there are the parks, and at most one or two smart shopping streets in the West End. The *café* with its tables on the pavement, indeed any form of *café*, is also unknown in London. The restaurants have no windows on the street, or if they have, they cover them up, because people do not like eating in full view of the world ; the bars always have separate compartments which divide their patrons from each other as far as possible, and if a house does possess a balcony looking on to the street, you may be sure it will not be used. The Englishman is averse from any enforced publicity, and the streets are for him a tiresome necessity not an amusement as they are to the Latin. It is only in the East End and other poor quarters that there is any street life in the sense that there is in continental towns, and there it exists—especially on Saturday nights—because the inhabitants lack the means of securing privacy.

The most characteristic thing that English town life has created is the club, and the very slight development of club life on the Continent is no less characteristic. The club is the corrective for individualism, a compromise between private life and community life in the shape of a carefully sifted community of people of like position or like mind. The London clubs are innumerable and of every conceivable kind—big political clubs, military, diplomatic and learned clubs, university clubs, purely social clubs, women's clubs and mixed clubs, athletic clubs in endless variety, and so on ; even night life is almost entirely confined to night clubs, of which there is an immense number, ranging from the extremely smart to the most dubious, from the most exclusive down to those which will admit anyone on payment of entrance money. All these clubs are withdrawn from the gaze of the curious : hence the sharp contrast in the look of the streets between London and Paris, the most typical continental capital. Paris gives the impression of being full of people taking the air and walking about the streets for fun, London of being full of workers hurrying to business or coming away from it. The impression is misleading in both cases: the Parisian has longer hours of work and less leisure than the Londoner, but he spends a large part of that leisure in the streets and *café*, while the Londoner disappears at once into the privacy of his home.

There is nothing gay or brightly coloured about a London street, yet it has an overpowering grandeur of its own and a mighty rhythm. London is not gay, but it is not frantically hurried or hysterical : though the traffic is as dense as in New York, it does not career madly through the streets but flows on in a never-ending, mighty but not unmeasured stream, with something of the inexorableness of a force of nature. In spite of its vast crowds and enormous motor traffic, London is not noisy ; the effect is one of a continual subdued humming coming from it as from the frictionless working of the engines of a vast liner. Well oiled and damped down, the traffic is controlled by the police, with apparent ease, by means of slight movements of the hands and seems to regulate itself automatically through the orderliness of the crowds. These crowds are a monotonous spectacle : all classes of society dress in much the same way, which is becoming more and more the case on the Continent too—the poor only being distinguished from the rich by the shabbiness of their clothes ; and yet even the most eccentric appearance fails to attract attention, because people are so used to exotics of every kind that no one so much as turns round to look at them.

The Londoner is a real Cosmopolitan for whom *nil admirari* is not a principle but a birthright. It never occurs to him to be proud of this position or to try in any way to impress you with it, and the ingenuous prattle of the New Yorker or the Berliner about the size of his city and its traffic, monster stores, hotels and shops is beyond his comprehension ; if he gives a thought to that sort of thing at all he is more likely to regard it as a necessary evil, and in any case he does not know the size of his city, which is far too vast to breed local patriotism. When gigantic buildings of the American type shoot up into the air as they have been doing in the last few years, they either pass unnoticed or arouse distaste ; London harbours an international exhibition like Wembley, but the Londoner is hardly aware of it ; the General Strike scarcely touched the surface of the place, and even the Great War hardly made any difference in its daily life. Londoners scarcely notice how quickly and constantly the general aspect of their city is changing, especially since the War. London has very little respect for its buildings—too little ; Regent Street, a unique architectural whole dating from the beginning of the nineteenth century, has been completely rebuilt in the last few years and has lost all distinction, and the unity of lovely old squares gets ruthlessly broken up by new buildings. The Englishman has no feeling for the beauty of the town, only for the beauty of the country ; so he has no scruples about destroying monuments of architecture, but is up in arms as soon as anyone proposes to fell a tree. Beauty and Town are to him mutually exclusive concepts and he is quite blind to the beauty of his own metropolis.

Is London beautiful? Not at all in the sense in which Paris is beautiful, i.e. on account of its splendidly laid-out streets and *places* and the unity of style in its chief thoroughfares. Paris has a classic beauty which no one can deny, London's beauty is like the face of a Rembrandt portrait ; it looks beautiful without being so. London gets its beauty from the climate, the light and, above all, the mist ; it is barely the same for two days, nay two hours, together, and is at its unloveliest in ' lovely ' weather. You get the most marvellous sunsets in the world on the river, lighting up with a magical radiance the masts and warehouses and bridges and towers that pierce the misty sky. Rain and mist, the sky signs, the trains puffing out steam as they roll by, the many-coloured reflections of a thousand lights on the asphalt are among the ingredients of London's beauty, and the soot that blackens every building, leaving only the turrets and domes standing out in their whiteness, the red of the innumerable buses against the grey of the streets, the flickering acetylene lamps in the street markets help to complete the picture. London's greatest charm is, above all, its incredible variety, its conglomeration of ancient and modern, high and low, in every conceivable style, of drab business streets and monastic houses withdrawn from the world, of the height of elegance and the depths of poverty, combining the characteristic of a great cosmopolitan capital, a small town and the country.

London's beauty is there for him who has eyes to see ; he will not find it starred in Baedeker, who, indeed, has but little to say about it—a dozen churches or fine buildings, the galleries and the parks, and that is all. The parks are the only one of the beauties of London that the Londoner really cares about ; for they are bits of the country, his Paradise Lost, in town. It is the gardens, squares and parks that reconcile him to his city : the garden behind his house, though often tiny, is his very own bit of country. The square is as characteristic a feature of London as the club, representing, like it, a compromise between private life and community life. The big square space is bordered by houses of the same size inhabited by people of the same class; the middle, just leaving room for the street, consists of a railed-in garden with lovely lawns, old trees, flower-beds and, in many cases, tennis courts, forming a miniature park, only open to the residents in the square, which provides a select community life screened from the gaze of passers-by by elder and laburnum, verdant trees and bushes.

Completely open to the public are the parks, in which London is very rich, each with its own character and particular charm. St. James's Park and the Green Park, being small, owe their effectiveness primarily to the palaces surrounding them, Hyde Park to its flowers, its fashionable life and its wide prospects of lawn and lake. Kensington Gardens are a bit of English Rococo, with their old straight walks, lovely lawns and carefully laid-out water gardens. Regent's Park is partly Classical in style like the streets round it, partly a bit of country with grass-land and trees and pasturing sheep, and so big that Zoological Gardens and a Botanical Garden can be hidden away in it. Next to it is Primrose Hill, one of London's innumerable hills, which forms an oasis undisturbed by the builder in the midst of the desert of stone. Further north are the open heath and hill country of Hampstead, beyond which the town has long ago closed in again. Battersea Park has the river and the biggest play-grounds. Kew Gardens, with the loveliest flowers and plants in the world, is a place of quite fantastic beauty such as a Humanity made up entirely of the prize specimens of every race would have. Richmond Park is a tract of woodland where nature is still wild but not savage ; Hampton Court and Bushy Park are London's Gardens of Versailles ; while Greenwich, at its opposite end, is a Park of Lenôtre's sloping up the hill and losing itself in the Heath.

It is impossible to make a complete list of the parks, commons, woods and heaths that form part of London's vast area ; impossible, too, to think of the town without these bits of country ; for it is only the two things together that give you London, the hotch-potch of everything that is to be found in England. Of course Continental towns have beautiful parks and gardens too, only none of their inhabitants have the Londoner's knowledge of how to make use of them. The Tuileries and the Luxembourg and the Thiergarten in Berlin are well-kept ornamental gardens where one has to ' keep off the grass ' but may walk on the intersecting paved or gravel paths or sit by the side of them ; one never loses the feeling of being in town. In a London park one gets the country ; people lie, sit and stroll about all over its green expanse, and the railed-off bits of ornamental garden are few and far between. The London gardener, like the Japanese, understands the value of the empty space and the wide expanse with only an occasional group of trees fanned by unhampered breezes.

Hyde Park, which is used by all classes of the community, is a particularly good example of what the parks mean to the population of London. It contains the Row, Society's riding-track, surrounded by expanses of grass where people sit on hundreds of comfortable chairs seeing what they can see ; this is the scene of the Sunday morning Church Parade and its fashionable glories. It also has tea-gardens and military-band concerts patronized by the middle classes, like a

Continental Spa, its lake for bathing, its ornamental gardens and its wide expanse of grass on which idlers and unemployed dream their days away. Finally, it is London's Forum, particularly on Sundays, on which day meeting borders on meeting on the North side. The big political and religious organizations send speakers to win support for their views, but anyone whom the spirit moves and who can find an audience to listen to him may speak. Next-door to the representatives of the Catholic Church or the Salvation Army, the Communists or the arch-Conservatives, you may listen to enthusiasts preaching the most peculiar gospels ; one man sees salvation in Esperanto, another in the prevention of vivisection ; here the topic is the question whether the English are the Lost Ten Tribes (which would make Christ, in a way, a British Possession) ; over there it is the sins of society. Among the speakers are Negroes and Indians, believers and atheists, revolutionaries and staunch servants of the established order : they must all be prepared to answer objections, but no one is refused a hearing. I know of no more impressive spectacle than this tolerance of the crowd for any and every opinion, and nothing more typically and exclusively English than these open-air meetings in the London parks.

It stands to reason in England that there is not a garden, square or park that does not in some way serve the interests of sport, though specialization and commercialization have naturally long ago caused each department of sport to construct its own Mecca— Ranelagh and Hurlingham for polo, Wimbledon for tennis, Lord's for cricket, and so on. The race-courses are very far out, some of them outside the widest boundaries of London. For aquatic sports there is the river, which is quite narrow above London and on a

Sunday in the fine season, with its innumerable punts, canoes, house-boats, gardens, villas, flower-beds and restaurants, presents a miraculous blending of town and country such as can be found perhaps nowhere else but on the Alster at Hamburg.

Gardens and parks, the river and the adjacent coast form the background of the Londoner's Sunday. No English institution enjoys a more unenviable notoriety among foreigners than the English Sunday, and this seems to have blinded people to the way in which the continental Sunday has grown to resemble the English one, and, conversely, to the enormous changes that have come over the Londoner's Sunday. What is its underlying principle? It is that Sunday shall be different from week days, shall be, in fact, a holiday. The foundations of the idea are of course religious, but the completely free-thinking social reformers of every country have raised the same demand as the Church for a day of rest, which is absolutely essential to the life of a great city. Sunday in London is a real restorative: for twenty-four hours the roar of the traffic is stilled, the streets are empty, the business quarters dead, and even the pavements give one the impression of enjoying their rest. The idea that there are no 'amusements' in London on Sunday has long been out-of-date; true, the great day of frenzied jollification is Saturday, on which all offices etc. shut as early as one o'clock, but cinemas and concerts go on as usual, and, though the theatres are shut, the 'Stage Societies' give their performances on Sundays, and there are Gala Dinners etc. at the restaurants. But even if these amusements failed, it would not be such a terrible disaster, because the Londoner's Sunday is consecrated to the country. The well-to-do (which in this context comprises a very large class) have created the week-end, which takes them into the country from Saturday to Monday, to big houses or little cottages, hotels or houseboats, on motor tours or in camps, as means and the time of year dictate ; at the very least everybody has his Sunday to himself, and everything is done to facilitate getting out of town ; the Sunday trains on the railways and tubes are different from the week-day ones, and innumerable buses run a long way into the country and as far as the sea, while even the poorest can get as far as Hampstead Heath or Richmond Park. London is quite as much alive on Sunday as on other days, only the scene of action has shifted from the centre to the circumference : if it has, on the whole, a remarkable 'steady' population, it has the English Sunday to thank for it.

Comparisons are pointless. When the Parisian, who has brought the town and town life to the highest pitch of development, goes into the country, whether it is in the neighbourhood or to a Spa, he rates it higher the more towny and like Paris it is; for he prefers living in a crowd. The Londoner's ideal being the country, he has built his city in such a way that he can forget it, by crowding its essentially urban features together into the streets and districts given over to business or amusements and keeping the residential quarters and their houses quiet and full of green. Streets, traffic, living in a crowd are a necessity from which he escapes wherever and whenever he can ; in town he is only half alive, and he would like best not to live there at all ; he has therefore created something unlike any continental city and unique in its kind, even more intensely urban in its treeless, cramped and overcrowded business quarters, the reverse of urban in its residential quarters, which have developed their own style, village-like in its suburbs, studded with parks, stretches of heath and green hills that have remained country. Infinite in extent, exceedingly many-sided, London is not to be brought under any formula and is hence ever new ; even for those that know her well, she is full of secrets and mysteries, a mighty Sphinx soot-blackened as Cleopatra's needle on the Embankment, the more herself the more she hides behind her veil, the most improbable and fantastic of the works of men's hands on this earth.

VII

OXFORD AND CAMBRIDGE

The two university towns of Oxford and Cambridge are not only of interest because they are among the finest towns in England, in Europe in fact, but also because they are unlike any others, with a quite peculiar character of their own, the study of which gives one an insight into the inner mysteries of England. Oxford and Cambridge are not merely charming and picturesque sights; they are highly significant institutions, and like the product of their training, the Oxford or Cambridge man, they stand for something. They have nothing in common with what is called a university town on the Continent, or rather, they are the only surviving university towns. The great universities of the Continent are situated in the capitals and hardly play any part in their life; in smaller towns, such as Heidelberg, they are naturally more important, but even a town like Heidelberg is not essentially different from other towns either in its outlook or its life. In Oxford and Cambridge the town is merely an extraneous appendage of the University; but the University is not a university at all in the continental sense: Oxford and Cambridge have no centralized University buildings, and there is a Cambridge story of a foreigner's taking a taxi at the station and telling the man to drive to the University, whereupon the man replied, perfectly correctly, 'There's no university here.'

The continental university is a large building, or

buildings, containing schools, lecture-rooms and laboratories, and frequented by students who come there to acquire some kind of knowledge and when they have acquired it will receive an official certificate of their having done so : for the rest, they live in furnished rooms or boarding-houses and share in the life of the great city or small town as the case may be. The University does not concern itself with the student as a member of society at all, though that does not, of course, prevent professors and lecturers from doing so ; they, and the students too, are free to choose whether they will cultivate unofficial relations or not, and it is equally open to anybody to join in the life of the students. The continental universities are specialized schools of jurisprudence, medicine, theology and philosophy, on a par with other specialized technical schools, art schools and schools of music, which are equally purely teaching institutions. Of the English universities, on the other hand, it is scarcely an exaggeration to say that they regard the imparting of specific knowledge as a secondary affair. Law and medicine are not extensively studied at Oxford and Cambridge at all ; law students go to the Inns of Court, medical students to one of the numerous universities, of which London University is the largest, which came into existence in the nineteenth and twentieth centuries and have nothing in common with the two older universities. One really can study theology and philosophy at Oxford and Cambridge but even that is not the essential thing ; for they are institutions which regard it as their main business to form *men*.

England still retains an aristocratic ideal and is ruled by an upper class which realizes or purports to realize this ideal. The chief thing an Englishman demands of people in leading positions is that the should be gentlemen, not that they should have specialized knowledge. He has the greatest respect for the gentleman and very little for the specialist ; but the gentleman is a specialist in the art of ruling, which is the aim and object of the education of the young Englishman of the upper class, the education that begins at the great Public Schools like Eton, Winchester and the rest and is completed at Oxford and Cambridge. The degrees people get there stamp them as members of the ruling class and their significance as regards learning is quite a secondary consideration. They are not so much places of instruction as training-grounds, their object being to mould the students' characters and form young men who shall continue the traditions of the ruling class as they have been formed in the course of centuries, in correspondence with the ideals of the English race. This aim has never been consciously formulated and is not set forth in any curriculum, simply because it is an assumption that is taken for granted ; and the character of this young man that the University is to form has equally escaped delineation in any manifesto. No one has written a primer describing how to be a gentleman or answering the question ' What is a gentleman ? ' Public School and University education being, in the true English way, predominantly a matter of instinct, is for that reason, like the ideal it has before its eyes, extremely changeable and constantly adapting itself to the circumstances of the time.

Oxford and Cambridge consist of a number of colleges loosely grouped together, of which the oldest were founded in the thirteenth century as monastic schools and even the newest still retain much of that character, while all owe their existence to private founders not to the State. In origin they resemble all the ancient universities, and the student in the Renaissance period found the teaching carried on in the same language, Latin, and on the same lines in all the universities of Europe, whether it was Oxford, Padua, Bologna, Paris, Salamanca or Prague, all being originally clerical: but it is Oxford and Cambridge that have preserved the image of those times most faithfully. In recent years, it is true, the bond between the colleges and the central authority of the University has been drawn somewhat closer; the colleges, however, continue their existence as separate entities, and the undergraduate does not simply enter the University, but becomes a member of a still semi-monastic college. The University is governed by its Chancellor, Vice-Chancellor and officials, and also appoints professors who lecture and pursue their researches independently of the colleges; but the real teaching remains in the hands of the colleges.

The colleges were originally intended for the instruction of poor scholars, and it was not till the eighteenth century that it began to be the 'correct thing' to go to the University, and not till the nineteenth that they became what they are to-day—institutions for the education of the sons of the ruling class, while the tendency at the present day is in a democratic direction. In the Ages of Faith Oxford and Cambridge produced clerics, in the Renaissance scholars and humanists, in modern times capable governors, while the specialist has been a by-product in all periods. The great majority of the spiritual and intellectual leaders of the country in every age have had the advantage of finishing their education there, and while the aspect of those leaders has been changing imperceptibly all the time, the outward appearance of the colleges has remained the same. Their venerable walls are overgrown with ivy and creepers, and in the courts are ancient lawns on which infinite care has been spent; in many cases there are gardens and playing fields adjoining too. Everything is peaceful, well cared-for and harmonious—intense cultivation without luxury—and nobody, least of all an adolescent, can escape the influence of such surroundings. The undergraduate is an adolescent and is treated accordingly ; he is no longer at school, but his liberty is limited. At Oxford he lives in college for his first few terms at any rate, and then moves into licensed lodgings, at Cambridge the opposite is the rule. These licensed lodging-houses are under the control of the University authorities, who altogether have extensive jurisdiction over the whole town. Each undergraduate has two rooms in college which he arranges as he likes ; he is bound, in most cases, to take a certain number of meals in hall and to attend chapel and invariably to be in college by a certain hour of the night; his studies are regulated by one of the college tutors. Such are the limitations set upon his liberty.

The three or four years that the undergraduate spends at his college are supposed to turn the schoolboy into a young man who conforms to the ideal of the English gentleman ; that is what he comes up for, and book-learning only represents a part of it. This ideal, which has only gradually taken shape, is the product of successive layers of tradition and forms an epitome of the development of English civilization. The colleges were originally clerical educational establishments, as I have said earlier ; hence the clerical element in the education they provide. The heads of the colleges are many of them in orders and chapel is mostly compulsory; the cap and gown of academic dress are clerical, and though the Universities are open to all denominations, they are still Church of England establishments, the Church of England regarding itself as the legitimate successor of the Catholic Church. The upper classes in England are predominantly Church-of-England, while the Dissenters come from the lower-middle and working classes; hence the very close alliance of mutual support between the Established Church and the ruling class, which gives real significance to the apparently merely external religious basis of college life.

The expenses entailed are enough to show that Oxford and Cambridge are meant only for the sons of the upper, or at any rate the wealthy, classes; this exclusiveness is certainly mitigated by the large number of scholarships, but it is their underlying principle, as it is that of the Public Schools. There are, moreover, considerable differences in social standing between the colleges, as they are none of them obliged, not being State institutions, to admit a man who does not meet with their approval. The great families have generally gone to the same school and the same college for generations—tradition again— and in many cases the boy is put down for a certain school as soon as he is born, and later on for a college and a club, so that his education is laid down in advance. The fact that the successive generations of undergraduates always belong to the same class (though this class is, of course, constantly absorbing new blood) makes possible the preservation of a continuous tradition of social conventions, customs and manners and the maintenance of a spiritual atmosphere which nobody can escape. The freshman very soon learns what the code of his college allows or forbids. He is expected to maintain a certain standard of living; on the other hand all ostentatious parade of wealth is strongly discouraged: for the college is, within its aristocratic framework, highly democratic. Thus members of foreign or native royal families, of which there are nearly always a few about, enjoy no sort of special precedence, any more than there is, for instance, any distinction made between nobles and commoners.

College life teaches a man to respect the rights of the individual even in communal life. A characteristic and truly English little point is the custom known as 'sporting one's oak.' Each set of undergraduate rooms has its own entrance with two doors, an outer one of oak and an inner one, sometimes of green baize: if a man wants to be left alone he shuts the outer door and nobody will think of disturbing him ; thus, though he lives in the midst of several hundreds of his fellows, he can remain undisturbed in his rooms alone or in the company of his chosen friends. This common life and the mutual interchange of influences that it brings is undoubtedly the most essential part of university education. Undergraduates of similar tastes collect together, and there is always a vast number of clubs and societies which meet regularly to pursue their political, literary, sporting or artistic interests. Apart from the private organizations there are of course the more official clubs, especially the athletic ones, and, most important of all, the Union. The Union has one unique feature beside the usual club services, namely, its debates, in which the procedure of the Houses of Parliament is reproduced and the same questions are discussed as at Westminster, divisions being taken. The Union is an oratorical academy and an unsurpassed preparatory school for parliamentary life ; men of the first rank in politics like Asquith and Balfour, and intellectual leaders like Shaw and Chesterton, have gladly accepted invitations to speak at the Union. At present large numbers of the undergraduates are Labour and the whole country takes an interest in their political views ; for they are the Ministers, Members of Parliament and high officials of to-morrow.

Classical studies occupy a prominent place in the

teaching of Oxford and Cambridge, and their educational ideal is a humanistic one, the result of putting the Renaissance tradition on top of the clerical one. There is among the English upper classes a surprisingly large number of people who are familiar with the ancient world, can read both its languages fluently and, in many cases, compose or even write verses in them, for whom Homer and Plato are living forces, thanks to Public School and University education. The Classics are, as they always have been, the foundation of English education and, in spite of all the attacks that the Age of Science has launched against them and all complaints to the effect that this ideal is out of date in a technical and industrial age, Oxford and Cambridge have not deserted their traditional path. A large number of scientific institutions have of course been established, but, at Oxford at least, they have remained sideshows. The cultivation of natural science, like that of medicine and law, has fallen to the lot of the newer universities which have sprung up in so many big towns in England and Scotland in recent times. Mastery of the ancient languages and familiarity with the spirit of the ancient world is part of the ideal of the cultured Englishman, precisely because it is a 'useless' accomplishment ; practical vocational education, on the other hand, is no part of the training of character. Hence a man will often spend two or three years in Oxford or Cambridge and then take up his specialized studies at a modern university or at the Temple, if he is going to the Bar, or at one of the hospitals if he is going in for medicine.

An Oxford or Cambridge degree is regarded, and rightly, as stamping a man socially, a degree at one of the other universities as a certificate of expert knowledge in a certain department, a thing for which the Englishman has no more respect than he has for the expert knowledge of a tradesman or anybody else engaged in practical life. The valuing of personality above knowledge is a fundamental thing in the English character; an Englishman does not want to know what a candidate for a job has been taught, but what sort of a person he is—the opposite extreme from the usual German attitude. In Germany they go for the expert, the specialist, and in doing so overlook the man; advertisements in German newspapers are always on the look out for employees 'with long experience,' 'who have already filled similar posts' etc., so that one often asks oneself how anybody manages to start his career at all. Hence Germany produces excellent and thorough specialists who, if they have to change their professions, are generally unfit for anything else, while England produces men who, have not the same wealth of specialized knowledge but, instead of that, can get on in almost any profession, with that genius for improvisation which was shown, for instance, in the creation of the English army in the course of the World War. Undoubtedly both nations have much to learn from each other in this respect.

The clerical and humanistic basis of education in England naturally did not escape the influence of subsequent developments. First of all, Puritanism left its mark on it; this is most conspicuous in the academic attitude to the problems of sex, which is in strong contrast to the humanistic spirit of the Renaissance. One would have thought that morals were bound to be very lax in places where thousands of young men are gathered together, but there is absolutely nothing of the Latin Quarter about Oxford and Cambridge. Except on certain definite festive occasions women are not supposed to visit men in college; disorderly houses are out of bounds, and the University authorities, who have the power of expulsion from the town, keep a strict control of hotels, lodging-houses etc. Oxford and Cambridge are towns with no prostitutes, which sounds completely crazy at first hearing; yet the system survives in practice. In the first place, there are many loop-holes: they are both near London, especially in this age of motor cars, and the vacations are long and frequent. But quite apart from that, the young Englishman develops late and his education does all it can to keep his development back, with the result that the undergraduate is still half a schoolboy. As a matter of fact the average young Englishman has as much contempt as his seniors for the dissolute life, and indeed for every kind of unbridled licence; for, though he may refuse ever to talk about it, he has an ideal of chastity. One might perhaps expect homosexuality to be commoner at Oxford and Cambridge than it is in places where full liberty in matters of sex obtains, but I do not believe it is; I believe that the majority curb their natural impulses with all the severity that one takes for granted in the majority of young girls of the same class.

The most important aid in achieving this result, though of course it is not avowedly directed to that end, is athletics. This is a side of athletic activity that mostly receives little attention, but it is just the side that makes them an instrument of education on which the schools and universities lay the greatest stress and largely explains the incredible importance which attaches to them there, into the cause of which the Englishman does not seek to penetrate further. Athletics are a religion, the importance of which in the educational system began at the point where orthodox religious belief gave out as an instrument of education, namely, in the nineteenth century. Athletics created a new code of morals and honour with just as great a binding force for its believers as the ecclesiastical one it superseded. They form character and teach the team spirit, subordination, self-sacrifice for an ideal and esteem for one's rival ; thus the athletes of the War, the airmen, were invariably decent and almost friendly in their relations with their colleagues of the enemy nations.

The importance attached to athletics at the University seems grotesque if one looks at it without understanding and bearing in mind its educational effect ; but when that is grasped, their importance becomes intelligible, though one may still find it excessive. It is not the goal that matters here but the road that leads to it ; whether Oxford or Cambridge wins the Boat Race by a few seconds, whether one college or the other wins the football match is really of no importance—a view that would make most Englishmen's hair stand on end ; yet all the same every Englishman knows that it does not matter whether a man wins a game or not, but does matter that he is a good sportsman. What is important is that the young men should be ready to give things up and go into training, to lead strictly healthy lives avoiding every sort of excess and to sacrifice pleasure and personal freedom for an idea, irrespective of what the idea is ; for the man who is capable of this when it is a question of some athletic victory will show his real capability when a more important issue comes along. The athletic heroes of Oxford and Cambridge, the Blues, are qualified, according to the English view, for great positions, not because they have broken some record but because their characters have been formed. The Blue who is at the same time a good classical scholar is regarded as the highest type of all ; he is also probably the type that comes nearest to the Greek ideal of youth and one of the best and most harmoniously developed that the world to-day can show. Such a young man will have had neither the time nor the inclination to give way to sexual impulses : the psycho-analyst would say that his libido has been transferred to other spheres ; it is this transference of libido, apart from the purely physical effects of athletics—exhaustion, the effect of violent exercise, constant baths etc.—which must not be underrated either, that makes athletic education an education in chastity too. The interest that is devoted to one sphere is withdrawn from the other, and though the athlete is not invariably a Joseph, he is certain not to be a waster. Athletics are, then, both physically and mentally one of the most important vehicles of education at the universities ; but let there be no mistake about it, their moral significance depends entirely upon their being treated in this spirit ; the Greek Palaestra, not the record-breaking of American professionals, must be the model ; for as soon as the athlete makes a business of it, he loses all his heroic features. As for the crowds that watch the great professional sporting events, that no more makes them sportsmen than going to church makes a man a priest or going to the cinema a film-star.

The ideal at which the education of the older universities aims has been the object of constant attacks from various angles, most of them based on misunderstanding. People criticize them on the ground that they neglect natural science, that their education does not fit a man for any practical career, that they occupy themselves with the dead past instead of the living present, that they overestimate the importance of athletics and that they are undemocratic. All these critics are quite right, in the sense that their contentions correspond with the facts, but unfortunately they misunderstand the nature of the University. You cannot blame a race-horse for not being a cart-horse ; it is just a different sort of beast. Race-horses are a luxury, and so, if you like, are Oxford and Cambridge, just as all aristocratic institutions may be regarded as luxuries: it is, however, just this instinctive aristocratic ideal that has up to now been a special mark of England, and what makes the older universities so significant is that a closer investigation of them gives one an insight into the nature of that ideal of humanity which the Englishman has before his eyes and the way it has grown up. The function of the Public Schools and the older universities is to educate the upper class that governs the country; they are opposed in their innermost nature to the democratic character of the *gymnasium* or the modern university (it must be remembered that there are plenty of institutions of that type in England too) and aim at the breeding of a select human type, selection being the antithesis of equal rights. The Englishman is far too too much of an individualist to believe in Equality or really want it to come; in every department, vegetable, animal and human, he is a breeder of prize specimens, which can only be reared at the expense of the masses, and a thoroughbred minority is incompatible with equality for all. He is, however, also a man of compromise; he wants an aristocracy, but it must have democratic features; so he created the first democracy in Europe, but based it on aristocracy.

The upper class in England has retained its supremacy through all the centuries by constantly absorbing new blood. To-day it rests on a capitalistic basis. One has to be rich to belong to it, the requisite education alone being extremely expensive; but the new rich who associate with the aristocracy have to adopt its ideals, customs and way of life, and while the aristocracy has been permeated by plutocrats, these plutocrats, or their descendants, have become assimilated to the aristocracy. The most important factor in this process is undoubtedly the connexion of wealth with ownership of land and country life, which tend, as can be seen in all countries, to preserve the family; whereas the the rich who remained urban have in most cases declined again in wealth and position in the third or fourth generation. Though the English show great respect for wealth and property, wherein they are honester than most other people, riches are not for them an end in themselves but a means to the attainment of a position of consideration and prestige. In addition to these, riches carry with them the obligation to take part in public life and the service of the State. England keeps up its privileged class, but that class is not hermetically shut off from the rest of the nation; there is no hard and fast division between the nobility and the middle classes, and the greater part of the aristocracy is *bourgeois*.

Whether the English aristocratic ideal will show itself adaptable enough to resist the attacks of the proletariat or whether here also a compromise is possible, only the future can show. The time when the upper class kept control of the country through its two political parties is over, and the Labour Party is making great strides: it must, however, be borne in mind that the position, as even electoral figures will show, is not the same as it is on the Continent, in that by no means all working men support the Labour Party and that, conversely, its leaders include a number of aristocrats. It seems to me more likely that here too a process, possibly a rapid process, of evolution will lead to a considerable broadening of the basis of the aristocracy than that the aristocracy, and with it the age-long aristocratic ideal of England, will be dethroned and pass over into its opposite. It is my belief that the descendants of the working man of to-day who will be filling the Oxford and Cambridge colleges in a hundred years' time will by then be very like their present occupants. Decline and surrender of privileges from above, growth and acquisition of them from below, and constant revision of the balance of classes—such is, in my view, the law of England's social, political and economic development.

VIII

SOCIETY

THE word 'Society' with a capital 'S' and the concept attached to it cannot be rendered by any translation. No other language has an equivalent word, because the concept has no place in other countries. The French talk of the *monde* or the *grand monde*, but the leadership of the upper class these words denote is confined to social life; since the triumph of republican ideas it has had little political influence, and it has become largely internationalized too. The Germans have never had a Society but only castes and classes, e.g. Court circles, the nobility, Good *Bürgerlich* Society, learned circles etc., which mutually ignore each other; and to-day everything is in a state of flux. In England Society is a perfectly definite concept and there is no doubt who belongs to it; yet it is difficult to put into words: nevertheless, in order to understand England it is necessary to grasp the nature of Society, because it is the most powerful factor in the life of the nation and, down to the very latest times, the most influential in shaping its course.

The nobility forms the core of Society, but the two concepts do not by any means coincide. Nobility implies a title, but in England only the eldest son inherits it (the eldest son of a duke, marquess or earl bears one of the family's secondary titles in his father's lifetime as a 'courtesy title'), the others only bear the family name, which is, consequently, what counts.

As late as the eighteenth century, Society consisted only of such families, many of which, incidentally, never possessed or acquired a title, and formed a homogeneous social class, the class of the big landowners, which succeeded in maintaining itself for centuries through the law of primogeniture and was only added to in those comparatively rare cases where new titles, in conjunction with estates, were conferred, e.g. on great commanders, statesmen and illegitimate scions of the Royal Family, Charles II being notably responsible for the last-named form of accretion. In that period Society presents much the same picture as the nobility of the Continent, and has much the same significance ; but there is one very important difference : the English nobility had not become identified with the Court, and lived on their property to a greater extent, never losing their connection with their estates, which were mostly entailed. In the nineteenth century the picture changes completely on the Continent, not only on account of violent upheavals like the French Revolution, but above all because the prodigious growth of commerce and industry, from which the nobility scornfully held aloof, brought about the transfer of real power to the capitalists in so far as it was not still, in countries with absolute governments, in the hands of the monarchs. In England things took a different course. In spite of the fact that industrialization and the rapid rise of commerce reached their highest point there, in spite of the fact that agriculture, of which the big landowners were after all the representatives, completely lost its importance, Society succeeded in retaining its power : it made up its mind to face the necessary compromises and allied itself to the plutocracy but never surrendered to it.

Reverence for everything that has tradition and breeding and a long history behind it is so strongly ingrained in the English character that an appeal to it never fails. The new wielders of power could think of no higher aim than to place their influence at the disposal of Society in return for being allowed to blend with it, and Society grasped the necessity, which the continental nobility had never grasped, of making this concession. So it incorporated the new material into itself, hesitatingly at first, then with ever-increasing eagerness; numerous new titles were conferred, and inter-marriage with the newly risen class began; merchants and industrialists, brewers and newspaper magnates, American and Jewish millionaires were received into Society, and Society soon learnt to take an advantageous part in their businesses. It lost some of its exclusiveness, but not its power of selection by any means, and achieved its object, i.e. retained its dominant position in the country; not more than a couple of dozen new families had been admitted to share in that position, and they, like all neophytes, were the most zealous champions of the position and privileges of the class among which they were now in a position to count themselves. Society has covered England with a network, each county having its island of exclusive Society, but its centre is London in the Season. It has no interest in the life of the big commercial and industrial towns and, although they contain a large proportion of England's wealth, especially in the Midlands, has no relations with it. The big manufacturers, tradesmen etc. of these towns belong to the middle classes; they remain town-dwellers—a decisive point—and do not accept the aristocratic ideal of living, and however important they may be from the economic point of view, socially they are non-existent.

Society has two aspects, the spectacular and the governing, of which the former is talked about a great deal, the latter only mentioned by its opponents. The interest which the whole nation takes in Society is astonishing. In continental countries, for all their *snobisme* and reverence for the nobility, the masses know very little about the 'best people,' who remain private individuals ; in England people in Society are public characters. Every newspaper tells you about their private lives, every illustrated paper is perpetually publishing photographs of them, and they are as much popular figures as cinema-actors are. Their parties and their dresses, their weddings, christenings and funerals, their houses and their travels are all described and depicted. It is difficult to say whether this is due to a conscious effort to make Society popular or whether the great public simply demands it ; but there is no doubt that the cheapest and most widely circulated papers, which are entirely adapted to the taste of the masses, pay the most zealous attention to Society. It is above all the vast lower middle classes that are most passionately interested to hear what sort of dress the Duchess was wearing, what His Lordship's favourite sport is and who the Bishop's wife was before she married. It is hard to determine how far this interest has penetrated into the working classes ; in any case they nearly all read the Rothermere or Beaverbrook papers which are chock-full of this sort of information ; there is only one Socialist daily paper, the *Daily Herald*, and it has a small circulation.[1]

All this interminable Society news and gossip only concerns its spectacular side. The first duty of Society is to be a show for the masses, particularly during the three months of the London Season, when it has not a moment's rest. There are the Court functions to be attended (incidentally the Court is far less exclusive and more democratic than Society, distinguishing between official functions, which may be attended by a wide range of

[1] Written before the recent reorganization of the *Daily Herald*.

people, and its private social life, where only people in Society come into the picture); then Society has itself to give dances, garden parties and receptions, which are announced and reported, and the Season is the time for important weddings; it has to patronize art by attending the opening of the Academy, in which the portraits of its members form the chief attraction; to be seen at first nights and fill the boxes at the Opera, which are all subscribed, ride or walk in the Park, go to the Horse Show and the Eton and Harrow match, put in an appearance at the big race-meetings, particularly Ascot and Goodwood, and watch polo at Ranelagh or Hurlingham, open flower shows and go to charity fêtes—in fact to carry out each day a spectacular programme quite beyond human powers, until it is finally allowed to leave London and, after duly going to Cowes, to devote itself, according to programme, to the destruction in the name of sport of the birds of the air in Scotland or on its estates, unless it happens to prefer to fly to the Continent, where its favourite spots are the recognized paradise of the snobs of all nations, places like Cannes, Biarritz, Le Touquet, the Engadine (especially in the winter), Cairo, Taormina and the rest owing their fame to English Society. All these social events and functions and journeys are chances for ordinary mortals to see and admire the Elect, and the Press caters in word and picture for those who cannot be there. It is simply the technique for making a monarch popular, as practised in the German Empire, Italy under Mussolini or Russia under Lenin, extended to a whole class. The key to the mystery, the unconscious ground of this apparently incomprehensible pre-occupation with Society in people who will never come into contact with the objects of their ardent interest (the American's interest in his plutocrats is just the same and has the same foundation) is this : Society is the real monarch in England, the King is merely a figurehead.

Everyone knows that Great Britain is a constitutional monarchy, but the Constitution has never been drawn up in articles. It is not the few written laws that matter ; indeed they are frequently at variance with the actual position ; the country is run on a compromise, always open to modification, between tradition, convention and the needs of the situation at any given moment. The significance of the monarchy depends on that of the monarch's personality. Antiquated laws give him powers which he would not in any circumstances be permitted to exercise ; in practice he says or puts his name to what the Cabinet approves, but nobody can prevent him from influencing the individual members of the Cabinet if he is up to doing so. The monarchical position of Society is equally vague and fluctuating and completely without relation to the written law : its only constitutional privilege is the institution of the House of Lords, which, however, ceased to count when it lost its Veto ; now it is bound to pass any measure that is again submitted to it in spite of two rejections. The real power of Society rests not on any constitutional powers but on its control over the whole machinery of government. Its influence is decisive in the filling of all the important positions, for most of which only men who belong to it by birth are considered. A Public School and University education is an indispensable condition ; only the highest abilities can make their way without it, and the people in control are clever enough to let such exceptions through. The higher official posts fall to the sons of Society, who fill the Foreign Office and the Embassies and Legations and govern the Colonies ; but Society understands the art of making talented individuals serve its interests and ideals by taking them up ; so Disraeli is made Lord Beaconsfield, Rufus Isaacs Lord Reading and Viceroy of India, and Chamberlain, a Birmingham manufacturer, becomes the champion of the aristocratic point of view.

All the important people who represent England abroad belong by birth or co-option to Society ; the great majority of judges and law-officers, the bishops and higher clergy of the Established Church, the holders of the higher commands in the army and navy, are all drawn from its ranks, except where they have gained their position through quite exceptional abilities. The important posts in every department of the Public Service all get filled by the younger title-less sons, the nephews, cousins and distant relatives of the aristocracy. Society is a club or secret society wielding a decisive influence in the public life of the country : the only breach in the walls of this stronghold is the House of Commons, the members of which have been drawn from all ranks of society since the extension of the franchise, the abolition of plural voting, the growth of the Labour Party, and so on. Consequently the chief ministerial posts tend more and more to be filled by people of relatively obscure origin : men like Asquith or Lloyd George, MacDonald or Birkenhead do not naturally belong to Society. This legislative side of the government, which is the side most in the public eye, works in accordance with democratic principles, and the influence which Society exercises on it is like the King's, personal ; but the administrative side, which is much less talked about and remains withdrawn from the control of public opinion, is the preserve of Society. Ministers change, but the permanent official goes on : who outside the inner ring knows the names of the people in the Foreign Office and the other principal government expected to satisfy the popular craving for romance. The King driving to the opening of Parliament in his gilded coach and the Peers in their coronets and ermine constitute a welcome pageant for the populace, the more so as they know, or rather, think they know, that these splendid figures have no real power. In any case the last thing the average Englishman wants is to abolish the display of the Great ; he is much more likely to dream of being one of them himself. On this attitude of mind rests the traditional social order of England, in which respect that of America resembles it ; there the place of the aristocracy is taken by the millionaire 'kings,' who in fact do their best to imitate it, and the ordinary American, so far from hating them, takes a pleasure in the contemplation of their doings and activities, confident that the way to those heights lies open to him too. The Englishman's attitude to his social superiors is quite different from the Frenchman's, for instance. The Englishman says to himself, ' I am as good as he is and there's nothing to stop my rising to his level ' ; the Frenchman says, ' He is no better than I am and therefore has no business to be above me.' The former wants to belong to the ruling class himself, the latter cannot tolerate the existence of a ruling class at all ; but the Englishman would not tolerate one that made a principle of its exclusiveness or even so much as laid stress on it. Even if he belongs to Society he would probably refuse altogether to admit the reality of its power, and for the reason that he takes it so much for granted that he is unaware of it. He is only aware of the privileges and prerogatives that the aristocracy has lost in the course of centuries, of the distance that democratic ideas have travelled and the extent of their conquests, and does not notice that this Democracy of his is under aristocratic leadership. He only has eyes for the brilliant façade of Society and misses its true significance.

Society on its side does all it can to preserve the appearance of extreme democracy. It is still, however, an open question whether the Englishman of the masses, if he saw things as they really are, as large sections of the proletariat after all do, would desire to see them radically altered or merely modified. The existing system has overwhelming testimony in its favour in the position of England among the nations, her Empire and her wealth, quite apart from motives of sentiment. The English aristocracy has proved its title as a ruling class; it may have feathered its own nest in the process, but it has brought the whole country to a position of eminence. The French and the Russian revolutions came when the Court and the upper class had brought ruin on their country and its people, and the present state of affairs in England offers no parallel to that, extremely serious as her economic and political difficulties are. In the exercise of its sway Society has always at the same time been the servant of the public and the common weal: the great families of England have been loyal to the fundamental principle of *noblesse oblige*, and have been leaders and servants of the nation, both in small things as landlords and owners of great houses, distributors of patronage and Justices of the Peace, and in great affairs as statesmen, diplomats, colonial governors, judges and so on. That is why the nation has greater confidence in them than in men of the middle or lower classes. A family like the Cecils, for instance, which has given great statesmen to the nation from the days of Elizabeth down to the present (Arthur Balfour, Lord Robert Cecil), has the same sort of prestige as an old-established firm with an unbroken record of first-class work has in other spheres. No new-comer can compete with them ; a man like Lloyd George, in spite of his services to the working classes as the introducer of Old-Age Pensions, National Health Insurance, socialistic agrarian legislation etc., has never possessed the confidence of the multitude ; he is too unstable, there is too much of the clever lawyer about him and too little character ; in fine, he is not a gentleman. Character and more character is what the Englishman demands of his country's leaders, and aristocratic tradition and training are the only warranty of character in which he really feels confidence. Society will make up its mind to broaden its basis and admit new blood on tactical considerations much more readily than the general public will consent to have the same respect for these new-comers, who find themselves in a prodigiously difficult position in relation to it and have to overcome a heavy weight of suspicion. The first Labour Government had far more difficulty with its own supporters than with the Opposition.

When one is dealing with people who stand at the head of affairs in virtue of birth, rank and wealth, one knows that they are not out for personal advantage ; with anyone else one can never be sure. As long as an aristocracy maintains its independence and its wealth, it inspires confidence as the servant of its country. By legislation and compromise English Society has succeeded in preserving its independent position and has never sunk into an appendage of the Court or shirked its duties ; and in contrast to all other aristocracies it has had the sense to come to terms with the aspiring middle classes and to bring the character of aristocracy into line with the character of the age. To-day it is exposed to bitter attacks, as it has so often been in the course of its history. Judging by the books and plays that deal with it, there is only one possible conclusion

—that it is utterly decadent and played-out. In these the life of the pleasure-loving Society people who constitute the Smart Set in London and the country-houses is painted in the most lurid colours, with adultery, drink and gambling, jazz, cocktails and the gramophone as their only occupations. Books and plays of this kind are immensely popular and not least so in Society itself, but their significance should not be over-rated ; they are simply the *chronique scandaleuse* that inevitably goes with any position of privilege. Not until the general public's burning interest in these topics is replaced by complete indifference—who in France, for instance, bothers about what goes on behind the scenes in the Faubourg Saint Germain ?—will the position of Society be in danger.

The Labour Party is, however, a serious threat to its influence on the government of the country. The political life of England has in the past been determined by the two-party system, and neither of the two old parties represented any particular class. It is true that there were more members of aristocratic society among the Conservatives and more middle-class people among the Liberals, but this rule had too many exceptions to count as a rule : membership of a party was always largely a matter of tradition, many great families having been Liberal for generations just as others had been Conservative. The Liberals were by tradition Free Traders, with a tendency to pacifism and 'Little-Englandism'; the Conservatives Protectionists, with a tendency to Imperialism— these were the differences of outlook that made a man plump for one party or the other. They were rivals, like Oxford and Cambridge, or Eton and Harrow, two teams from the same club playing each other ; for behind the party game stood the guiding force of Society, the great Club, some of whose members wore white and others red. Thus both parties served one and the same master; but Socialism demanded the representation of the working classes by members of the working classes; it consciously stood for the interests of a class. This demand and this class policy are nothing like so violent as they are, for instance, in Germany, the cradle of Social Democracy, and election figures are enough to show that even to-day a large proportion of the working classes vote for the older parties; but the mere principle of the thing is a declaration of war against the old English parliamentary system. The growth of Labour having taken place chiefly at the expense of the Liberals, there will soon again be two parties facing each other, the Conservatives and the Labour Party. The question then is whether it will come to a cleavage between Haves and the Have-Nots, which would mean the end of government by Society, or whether the Labour Party will develop into an Opposition in the old sense, to take the place of the Liberals. As far as one can see, the latter is more likely to happen. All the efforts of Society are of course directed to this end, and, having once recognized the strength of its opponent, it is ready to make any concession, as long as the principle at stake remains inviolate. The Labour Party already contains many members belonging by birth to Society; the first Labour Cabinet conformed to all the traditions, from the Prime Minister's Court dress onwards, and we have seen the King represented in Scotland by a miner and his wife and the highest in the land forming his temporary Court. A great many things are thinkable in England that would be impossible elsewhere, and the logically inconceivable is none the less perfectly possible if only it stands the test of practice. Compromise with the lower classes may come off as compromise with the middle classes did. One thing is certain : if it does not, England will be faced with the greatest internal upheaval she has known for many centuries ; if on the other hand it does, groups of extremists will separate off both on the Right and on the Left, but they will have no influence and the existing system will survive.

Analogies from continental countries, it cannot be repeated too often, are misleading. England has no clique of nobles bent on conducting affairs in the narrowly conceived interests of the landowners and their supporters or of the Court contrary to the will of the majority, such as the old German Conservatives, for example, were ; nor has it a clique of aristocrats and capitalists making Parliament and the administration subservient to its interests by secret corruption, such as exists in most of the 'free' republics. No doubt there are features here and there in the situation in England which agree with those just described, but they are not the essential ones ; in the case of England's ruling class, the point at issue is its right to govern. In practice it governs, to the best of its knowledge and ability, in the general interest ; that it does not neglect its own follows from the fact that it consists of human beings and not of saints ; but it is only fair to admit that it takes its duties quite as seriously as its rights and has always been prepared to make the greatest sacrifices. In other countries too the upper classes have offered up their children in time of war, but only in England have they offered up their money in the same way. The rich were already paying enormous taxes long before the Labour Party had attained to any importance, and they are still paying them. Small incomes are untaxed, moderate ones are taxed lightly, big ones up to seventy per cent., and the position has long been the same in regard to death duties. This has meant that the expropriation of the upper classes has been going on for years under the aegis of Society, hitting the capitalist and the landowner equally, and so hard that there is scarcely a Socialist who could wish for more—all without disturbance to the economic life of the country as a whole.

This nameless multiple ruler of England conceives of its function much as Frederic the Great conceived of his royal office. One need not necessarily share its view that the privileges and duties of government belong to it by right ; for they are inherited privileges and duties and nothing more : but one cannot refuse respect to anyone who acts up to his convictions consistently, regardless of his own loss or gain. It is open to question whether the position of ruler is preferable to that of the ruled. The English brand of democracy, with an aristocracy to lead it and Society supreme in the background, has sprung from no principle and is compatible with no logical system, nor can it be transplanted to other countries or other conditions. It is a product of evolution, a natural organism which has developed in the course of the centuries. To a supporter of Mussolini it must seem full of democratic weaknesses, to the democratic republican an unjust class government, to the Communist a fit object for destruction, like everything else that stops short of the pure Dictatorship of the Proletariat. To the majority of Englishmen it is simply a natural fact on which they have never reflected : they would never use the word 'Society' in the sense in which I have been using it ; to them 'Society' is simply a brilliant pageant acted by people born to the part, and they are blind to its real significance. It is, however, open to question whether a recognition of its significance would shake their conviction that the English system is the right system for England. In these matters the English are given neither to fanaticism nor to enthusiasm. The Prime Minister in the last Government, in answer to a question in the House whether he was satisfied with the state of things in some department or other, replied that he could mention absolutely nothing in England with which he was satisfied. That is the real English attitude ; the Englishman thinks the same of the Government and the political system of the country as that Government thinks of itself ; that is, he thinks it far from ideal, but he has got to be satisfied that some other system would get nearer to the ideal before he will upset the existing one. Those that have been tried out in other countries have so far not satisfied him that they would, and it would have to go very, very hard with him and his country and uncommonly well with the countries under proletarian or military dictatorship before he would consider exchanging his system for one of theirs.

IX

POLITICAL POLICY

In politics the English have a world-wide reputation for treachery and hypocrisy, and *Perfide Albion* has become proverbial. One often hears the view expressed that, while the individual Englishman is a decent and reliable person, the English as a nation are none the less intriguing, dishonest and not to be trusted in politics. This view proceeds from the naïve assumption that there are nations which pursue an open-hearted altruistic policy in obedience to ethical or moral ideas. Up to now the statesman, of whatever nation, who aimed at advancing his own country's interest has advanced it at the expense of the interests of other countries; everywhere the leaders who directed foreign policy have been far removed from moral scruples, and their own country's advantage has taken precedence of any obligation or promise entered into or any legitimate interest of another country. The one decisive factor has everywhere been Might, and a latent state of war has reigned between nations, politics being a war carried on with the weapons of astuteness, intrigue and corruption. English policy has had exactly the same object as the policy of other countries, namely, the maximum aggrandisement of one's own nation, and its method has been the universal one of peaceful over-reaching and, where that failed, force of arms. It is only in the most recent times that the idea of subjecting the relations between nations to the same moral laws as are recognized, at least in theory, in the offices who really guide the policy and destiny of England? It is in every way probable that the Labour Party will in the course of a few years get a clear majority in the House of Commons and have things its own way there ; but it is very much less probable that the spirit of the administration will change : Society is extremely far-sighted ; many of its members already belong to the Labour Party, and a determined struggle has long been going on behind the scenes to make the party of the Workers, which is unlike either of the two historic parties in representing a definite class interest, into an Opposition in the old sense, ' His Majesty's most loyal opposition ' as it is officially called, i.e. Society's.

It would be giving a misleading picture of Society to represent it as a secret influence, the hidden hand behind the throne, shaping the country's course to its own advantage. We have not to deal here with a French nobility of the *ancien régime*, which plunders the people, pays no taxes and knows only privileges, no duties ; whose outlook on life is purely selfish and pleasure-loving. Society is representative of the true aristocratic principle, the case for which is just as plausible as the case for the democratic principle ; for both seek the welfare of the community and are only divided over the means of bringing it about. Society has a thoroughly English conviction of the superiority of the man to whose breeding heredity, tradition and education have contributed their best, and it regards itself, on the whole justifiably, as a highly bred class in that sense—not, that is, as constituting a higher type of humanity all round, but as specially developed and trained to be the best possible leaders and governors of the country, which it regards as a matter of character even more than as an art, believing that great gifts and intelligence can only outweigh the advantages of heredity and tradition in exceptional cases and quite honestly holding the rest of mankind unfit to govern. Its strength, however, lies in the fact that so far at least the majority of people in other classes quite instinctively share its view. This conviction is never formulated and there is no party officially standing for the aristocratic principle; but the ideal that Society has before its eyes is the ideal of very wide sections of the nation, which would only begin to show opposition if they considered themselves excluded from it; and the law of the land leaves the way open for everybody. The most important point, however, is that the existing system has stood the test of practice, which for the English is enough to turn the scales in its favour. They know that they have enjoyed better government and a juster administration than any other nation, and neither the corruption of democratic republics nor the inflexible regimentation of absolute monarchies could appear desirable to them; Bolshevist Russia is the only place that confronts the traditional English system with a rival one which portions of the population think better; that is why every possible weapon is being used to combat it.

The Englishman has great reverence for anything handed down by long tradition, and further, he adores anything picturesque—instincts which the ruling class is clever enough not to lose sight of. The masses value the pageant it provides for them and would hate to see it go; hence that continual parading on the part of Society, which is highly disagreeable to many individual members of it. All the display that surrounds the King, the Court and Society is at bottom a circus-parade for the benefit of the people. In private life the great ones of the earth are required to be quite ordinary folk aspiring to a simple and virtuous domesticity, like any Smith or Robinson; but in their public appearances they are relations of individuals, has begun to take root outside narrow pacifistic circles. The idea, incidentally first formulated by an Englishman, Norman Angell, that the interests of the nations are to-day so bound up with each other that even a 'victorious' war spells disaster, has become pretty general since 1918, and the League of Nations is the first hesitating attempt to translate the admitted truth into terms of practice. The new doctrine says 'The interests of the nations are in the main identical and the strength of A. depends on the strength of B.,' whereas the old doctrine said 'Their interests are opposed and the strength of A. depends on the weakness of B.' As long as the latter continues to prevail, it is simply childish to expect any nation's foreign policy to be anything but a ruthlessly waged underground war against its fellows.

International politics have always been untouched by morality everywhere, and in Europe they have always stood out in strong contrast to the ethics of Christianity which its nations professed. The political game consisted of the pursuit of increased power and possessions at the cost of one's neighbour ; it was only the pretext that varied ; sometimes it was the cause of Religion, sometimes the interests of the dynasty, sometimes those of the People. The policy of Philip II of Spain in the Netherlands was the same as that of Louis XIV in Alsace and the Palatinate or that of Frederic the Great in Silesia and over the partition of Poland—Frederic himself has left a most cynically frank judgment of his own policy in his correspondence—and Napoleon's aims differed no whit from those of his enemies. British policy is precisely the same as the policy of other countries and their Cabinets ; the most that can be said of it is that it has been more skilful and has known better how to achieve its ends peacefully and, when it got into difficulties in war, was most successful in getting other people to pull the chestnuts out of the fire. But as long as politics are what they have been, say what one may, up to the present, that is an excellent, a model policy, just as Bismarck's thoroughly perfidious Guarantee Pact was ; for perfidy is of the essence of politics. Yet conquest by force or fraud may subsequently justify itself : for instance, Frederic the Great managed to make a very different thing of the provinces he conquered from what Philip II made of his. Britain's colonial empire arose in the same manner as the Spanish ; the justification of her policy lies in the results it obtained. Being more intelligent and far-sighted, it was never a policy of plunder ; it took, but it also gave. As a far-sighted captain of industry cares for the welfare of his employees and pays good wages, so has England grasped the wisdom of treating the conquered well and dealing justly with them. Enlightened egoism—and herein lies the secret of success—has regard for other people and is not opposed to altruism ; the maxims of ethics are the reverse of unpractical.

If British policy is misjudged by most people on the Continent, the reason is that they look at it from the wrong angle, as the policy of a European state, of one of themselves. Great Britain's policy has for more than a century been primarily concerned with overseas affairs : European questions are not her first care, and the problems and interests of her continental cousins are not particularly near her heart ; she has other standards of greatness. Another thing that makes British policy difficult to understand is that, in conformity with the nature of the Englishman, instead of following any logically thought-out plan, it relies largely on intuition and is constantly adapting itself to circumstances. If the statesmanship of ancient Rome, whose empire was lovers of peace, who are, as I have said above, extremely numerous, and no English government would venture to-day to stand in the way of the unification of Europe, because the opposition in its own country would be too strong; all it would do would be to insist, quite justifiably, that a United Europe should not be allowed to come into existence without the consent and co-operation of England. The Realists in English politics, who mostly belong to the Conservative Party, would raise no opposition to this tendency on practical grounds: true, they do not believe in Peace, perhaps not even as an ideal to be aimed at; but even they want peace in Europe, because the objectives of British policy lie outside Europe and military entanglements on the Continent can only disturb them. England's chief interest lies in Asia and her chief enemy is Russia, whose influence she has to contend with in India, China, Persia, Turkey and right down to Egypt. She has drawn much closer to America, which has an even stronger anti-Bolshevist attitude, and on the other side has renewed her friendship with Japan, whose differences with America she is anxious to smooth out because they mean a weakening of the anti-Russian front. She has succeeded in getting Japan to hold aloof from the Pan-Asiatic movement directed against the colonial Powers, and she is fighting for supremacy in India and for every inch of ground in Asia with incredible pertinacity and all the resources of diplomacy. At the same time she is accomplishing extraordinary things in the Sudan in her efforts to build up her African Empire (e.g. the Cape-to-Cairo idea); Egypt is 'independent,' but the new Nile dam makes it dependent on the power that holds the Sudan, where vast cotton plantations are growing up. England has a monopoly of rubber and has secured oil fields of the first importance—in fact, she is pursuing a far-sighted policy.

The question of the future of the British Empire is unanswerable. That Empire is threatened at every corner, but so it always has been from the beginning. Its strength lies in its incredible elasticity : it is not iron but bamboo that is strong, said Lao-Tse. It could stand all sorts of amputations and probably survive even the loss of India without going under. It looks as if the rule of the Whites over the Natives were coming to an end, and the British Empire is based upon it ; but its fundamental basis is something far less palpable : like all real power, it is founded on an idea.

'Independence' of England is in many cases, considering the loose constitution of the Empire, a mere formula. The 'white' Dominions are bound to England by a consciousness of affinity, and even the others have up to now adopted English ideals and wanted, on their side, to attain to English liberty and English self-government—in short, to become as English as possible ; it is just because Bolshevism is striving to substitute another ideal for this one that it is such a danger to England. In spite of enmity and repulsion, the governing Englishman and the imperial 'white' country have so far been the model to which all their coloured dependents have striven to approximate, and the supersession of this ideal by another would constitute the first real threat to English dominion. The English are an extremely sound, tough and vital people, and their Empire is not tied to any formula ; even if the end of colonial dominion is bound to come some day, there are other possibilities : a union of the mother country with the 'white' Dominions of Canada, Australia and South Africa, a close combination with the United States, even a political union of all the countries of Anglo-Saxon culture, are all possibilities for the political future of Great Britain.

built up on a consistent plan, is reflected in the geometrical planning of Roman towns and streets, the growth of the British Empire is equally symbolized by the British metropolis, both being without plan, determined by chance external conditions and only assembled as an after-thought into a loose whole consisting of a medley of different-coloured parts thrown together. 'The Empire was founded in a fit of absent-mindedness' is an English saying. It is more of a natural growth than a deliberate structure. There is no system about English colonial policy ; it is determined by circumstances, and includes every degree of independence and self-government, from the Dominions of Australia, Canada, South Africa and, recently, Ireland, which are bound to the mother country by nothing but a common personal allegiance and certain contributions to Imperial Defence, to the Crown Colonies and Dependencies and down to the completely dependent colonies. India is a unique problem, part of it, British India, being entirely dependent and part ruled by native princes who vary very much in the degree of their independence. The whole Empire is a sort of League of Nations whose members do not by any means enjoy equal rights, and which can only be held together and governed by continual new compromises and modifications in view of continually changing circumstances. Spread over the whole earth, it is united by the sea, on the command of which its existence consequently depends. As far as numbers go, the Englishmen, nay the Whites altogether, form a tiny minority, large populations being governed by a handful of Englishmen—a fact which alone speaks for the skill of British statesmanship.

Even where the Englishman is not popular he is respected and his fairness and incorruptibility are admitted. He avoids all unnecessary interference and any sort of mixing with the coloured people in the Empire—this last being one of his very few unalterable principles. The relation between the Englishman and the inhabitants of the Colonies is much the same as that between the masses and the ruling class in England itself, the English constituting the 'Society' of the British Empire; within this principle of Inequality, which they take for granted as a fact, their government is laboriously just. In general the Colonies are gradually growing up to self-government; in one particular case, India, where England is afraid of a complete severance, she is seeking to put off the evil day as long as possible. No nation can desire or like the foreign yoke, but very few of those under British rule would prefer that of any other foreigner. England has in no sense simply sucked the Colonies dry; on the contrary, she has developed them, at her own expense in many cases: many colonial industries compete with those of England and are protected by tariffs while England lets their goods come in free of duty, and many of the Colonies compete hotly against each other in the same way.

Even in commerce, the British spirit is against system as long as there is any possibility of muddling through and shrinks from the inflexibility of the letter of the law. Hence that apparently tricky, incalculable and unreliable element in British statesmanship which the French or German mind finds incomprehensible and sinister. In 1918, after the collapse of the German Empire, if it had been English statesmen who had to find a new form of government they would certainly not have proclaimed a united German Republic. To the logical German mind, once the Monarchy had disappeared, the only possible form of government was the republican. Logically they are mutually exclusive, but facts seldom correspond with logic, and Germany is made up of various sorts of political structure: the Englishman would, in all probability, have cheerfully erected a non-monarchical whole in the shape of a Confederation of States, of which the parts would have continued as kingdoms, duchies, republics etc., as the case might be—he would, that is, have established a compromise which took into account the existing situation. The fundamental difference between British statesmanship and that of all the other nations of Europe is this, that the English take things as they find them and do their best to get them going with a minimum of friction, while the others start with an idea and try to force things to fit it: the Englishman lets the nature of things guide him, other people try to impress their spirit forcibly on things. With such different points of view they cannot understand each other's ways of doing things, and what makes British policy incomprehensible to the Continental is simply its lack of system.

All the same, it is not at all so difficult to understand. Though full of contradictions in details, it has been unswerving in its main lines for centuries. Continental nations regard England as perfidious because she knows nothing of traditional friendships or enmities and allies herself to-day with France against Germany, to-morrow with Germany against France, with republics against monarchies and with monarchies against republics, with Protestants against Catholics and with Catholics against Protestants, even with Infidels against Christians, quite as easily as the other way about. But that only means that she definitely does not allow herself to be deflected from her straight course by any principles. Her system is, No Principles; with other nations motives of sentiment play a greater part and are less easily set aside, though they have regrouped themselves often enough too. And when all's said and done, in their case the 'solidarity' of European monarchs, for instance, prevented neither wars between them nor such things as the partition of Poland: monarchical Russia allied herself with republican France, the Crescent was supported by Christian Powers against other Christian Powers; in short, reasons of State—in former days dynastic interests—have been decisive on the Continent too, in spite of the great influence of traditional friendships and enmities. The fact that these have no such influence on England's policy is explained by her insular position: England regards the Continent as a whole external to herself, all the parts of which are equally foreign. The countries of the Continent are moved by much stronger feelings, whether friendly or hostile, towards neighbouring countries than towards others; naturally, therefore, the Continental has a far greater variety of attitudes than the Englishman, whose view of everybody is equally objective.

England supports those who further her interests and fights those who stand in her way, and, having no hereditary friends or enemies, she can change both. Since the day when the destruction of the Armada laid the foundation of her command of the sea, the maintenance of that command, on which the existence of her Empire depends, has been at the bottom of every one of her political moves: everything else is secondary and derivative from that object, which alone determines her attitude to other Powers. Anyone who threatens England's command of the sea, and therefore any great European Power which could possibly set on foot an overwhelming coalition against her, and any independent Power holding the Flanders coast, is her enemy. Hence the necessity for England of maintaining the Balance of Power which keeps the strong nations in equilibrium, of preventing the coalition of any two great naval powers against her, and of keeping the Flanders coast in the hands of a dependent or neutral small nation. In addition to these, another motive has come into the picture in modern times, namely the retention of India, so far the most important pillar of Britain's world-power and the corner stone of the Empire, and anyone who threatens, or possibly could threaten, India is likewise England's enemy. These have been the clear and undeviating guiding-lines of British policy for centuries, and all the apparent mysteries, perfidies and changes of principle are easily intelligible in this light.

In reality British policy is the most consistent policy in the world, never failing for a moment to subordinate secondary issues to the main issue, without any regard for prestige, and continually sacrificing the interests of the parts (e.g. sovereignty, industry and trade) to the interest of the whole. Spain, Holland, France, Germany were all regarded as enemies by Great Britain the moment they threatened her command of the sea, and Louis XIV, Napoleon and the German Empire had to fight her according as they had achieved supremacy on the Continent or got near to that goal. She has always succeeded in getting together a coalition against her enemies, allying herself with Prussia, Russia and Austria against Napoleon, and with France, Russia and the rest against Germany with equal readiness. One nation is as good as another in her eyes, but she always remains true to herself. She is not aggressive and prefers peaceful methods, but she does not shrink from the risk of war in pursuing her major aims. From the time of Elizabeth to the Great War the same point of view has controlled her policy; it is only the details that are obscure, the main lines are clear as day. After the command of the sea, Britain's most vital interest is the retention of India. Now her only serious rival in Asia has been Russia. She supported Turkey against Russia to prevent her gaining possession of Constantinople; she allied herself with Japan against Russia, dismissing all those questions of equality between the white and the coloured races to which she attaches so much importance on other occasions; though Russia was her ally, she gave the Russian Revolution her blessing and looked with no unfavourable eye on Bolshevism in its early stages, as promising to weaken Russia for an indefinitely long time; it was not till Russia returned under a new banner to the struggle for Asia that she became its uncompromising foe.

Britain's foreign policy is clearer, less ambiguous and less variable than that of any other country, and the accusation of impenetrability and untrustworthiness comes from defective insight; nevertheless the charge of hypocrisy generally preferred against it is not without justification: it is hypocritical in as much as it keeps quiet about its true motives and intentions and conceals them behind a façade of High Morality. That is, of course, not in the least a British monopoly. For centuries all wars have been carried on by all parties concerned under more or less lying pretexts: Napoleon conquered Europe 'to bring it freedom'—after suppressing freedom in his own country; the Allies fought against him 'to deliver the nations from the foreign yoke' —for which they proceeded to substitute government by the police; and in the Great War every country without exception took the line that it had been forced into war by the enemy in spite of its efforts for peace. In short, any and every policy finds noble and highly moral grounds for itself; that does not, however, proceed from a love of hypocrisy but from the necessity of getting public opinion in one's own country on to one's side. The greater the influence and power of the masses, the greater the necessity of presenting things in the light in which they want to see them. Now the masses are always sentimental, never cynical. In this sense the atmosphere of falsehood that envelops politics is evidence (and a result) of democracy and the importance of public opinion, and since the power of public opinion is greater in England than in any other European country, it is there that the tissue of lies is most strongly and closely woven. Patriotic phrases are not sufficiently effective by themselves nor will prosaic arguments by any means satisfy the people, but it is very easy to bring them into line by an appeal to their ethical convictions, to their idealism : the White Man's Burden, his duty to bring civilization and just government to the coloured races, justifies many a colonial war that the masses would otherwise condemn. In England, where there is no conscription, the government has no power of forcing the nation into a war ; it has to adapt itself to the national character, in order that the People may be convinced that it is merely carrying out their wishes. Hence the British Cabinet's fear in 1914, even on the eve of the declaration of war, of entering into and acknowledging any binding agreement which public opinion would not forgive them. The violation of Belgian neutrality gave the government its first clear ground in the eyes of the masses for declaring war on Germany—namely, the defence of the weak against the strong and the sacredness of Great Britain's guarantee of the neutrality of Belgium.

The most powerful instrument for influencing public opinion, is, of course, the Press and its propaganda, and its methods never change and never fail. The lampoons against Napoleon and those against William II have the same contents, and the Russians were called Huns in the Crimean War long before the Germans in

1914; the enemy is invariably accused of the same utterly inhuman atrocities. No Press accomplished more monumental work in this line during the War than the English, especially the Northcliffe papers; but one has to remember how important it was for the government that hatred of the enemy should be instilled into the Englishman who was by nature so little inclined to it, 'friend' and 'foe' being alike foreign and indifferent to him, and to remember too that no English government could venture to muzzle the opposition by suppressing freedom of speech. There is always a large number of men—and women—in England who are ready to make any sacrifice for their convictions, and the government knows how dangerous it would be to make martyrs of them. Even the appeal to patriotism as the supreme duty and the necessity of refraining from all criticism as long as the country is in danger, fails to work in dealing with this type: thus Campbell-Bannerman, the leader of the Opposition during the Boer War, called the English conduct of the war barbarous and unworthy of a civilized nation and refused to be silenced, and in just the same way men like Shaw, Bertrand Russell, Keir Hardie and Morel and their supporters raised their voices against the Great War and its lies, while an unbroken protest rose from public meetings and articles in numerous newspapers, the conscientious objectors refused to fight, and so on. This strong opposition could not be suppressed, but everything possible was done to discredit it in the eyes of the public. The propaganda carried on by the Press was even more important inside England than abroad; for the darker the colours in which the enemy appeared, the more contemptible did the people who stood up for him or refused to fight against him look. Lies are a more essential ingredient in English policy than in any other country's because the passion for truth is greater, independence of judgment commoner and blind obedience rarer there: as long as politics are an affair of brute egoism, while the morality inculcated into the masses in peace time is that of Christian altruism, so long will there be no such thing as a policy free from mendacity and hypocrisy, and the more living and effective a force that morality is in any country, the greater will be the hypocrisy.

For centuries England has pursued but one object as far as Europe is concerned—namely, to prevent the formation of an overwhelming coalition against herself, and has worked against the unity of Europe, being the chief party interested in keeping it divided. And yet it seems to me a mistake to consider this attitude of hers to the problems of the Continent as final; in fact I think it is a thing of the past. England to-day is pacifist, not merely because the great increase of territory which the War has brought her has satisfied her appetite for a long time to come, but also because very large sections, particularly of the generation now growing up, are convinced of the senselessness of war, at least of a European war. With her trade and her industry in the doldrums as a result of the impoverishment of Europe, she has a strong interest in its reconstruction; that is what has made her the most zealous champion of the idea of the League of Nations. No doubt the ghost of her old continental policy, which would play off Italy against France and France against Germany, still stalks abroad even now, but that policy is doomed on various grounds, some of them ideal: the overwhelming majority of the English nation cherishes a genuine desire for peace, and the ever-growing Labour Party desires and promotes a united Europe as a basis for more far-reaching understandings. These motives are capital with all the sincere

X

THE FOREIGNER IN ENGLAND

The peculiar constitution of the British Empire and the peculiar character of the Englishman necessarily affect his attitude to the foreigners settled in England and to foreigners in general. This attitude is not easily defined, being, like every aspect of the national character, open to several interpretations. Before the War, England was the most hospitable of countries : no difficulty was put in the way of immigrants, and political exiles at all times found refuge there, with the result that England, and especially London, has an immense alien population. To-day there are more difficulties in the way of immigration, possibly as a temporary measure due to unemployment, but the attitude of the natives to the foreigners settled among them has not altered. London has a number of quarters inhabited almost exclusively by foreigners, but the fact, so far from provoking adverse criticism, is not even deemed worthy of attention : Frenchmen, Italians, Spaniards, Jews in large numbers, Chinese and Indians monopolize streets and whole districts ; only the German colony, which occupied an important position before the War, has almost disappeared. England was the most hospitable country of Europe—the position of the United States, as needing immigrants, was quite different ; France has also turned into a magnet for immigrants since the War. In England the aliens have settled down freely, transforming whole quarters of towns to their taste and preserving their customs, usages and languages, without a thought of resentment on the part of the natives. Toleration goes so far that in Whitechapel, for instance, the centre of the Eastern Jews, the laws for keeping Sunday a day of rest do not run and the shops shut on the Sabbath and are open on Sunday, which is the chief market-day in the week; the shop signs are in Hebrew letters there and in the theatres the plays are given in Yiddish. Similarly in Soho the signs and names of shops and restaurants are written in French and Italian, and in Limehouse in Chinese. One is tempted to think that a warmer welcome or greater freedom could not possibly be accorded to the foreigner, but a closer examination reveals the fact that this toleration and freedom have their reverse side: the foreigner in England enjoys every imaginable liberty but he always remains a foreigner; he is not required, as he is in other countries, to bow the knee to the spirit of the country, there is not a trace of compulsory assimilation; but, as against that, no foreigner, however perfectly assimilated, is ever accepted by the English as one of themselves.

In order to understand what the concept the word 'foreigner' conveys to the average Englishman, it is necessary to take a closer look at the foreigners settled in England. There are many Englishmen living on the Continent and many Continentals living in England; the difference is that the English living abroad are mostly well-to-do people who prefer living there for reasons of climate or society, while an immense proportion of the foreigners in England belong to the lowest classes. The Englishman goes abroad to spend money, the foreigner comes to England to earn it. To a foreigner the word 'Englishman' calls up a picture of a rich tourist (see the caricatures of the Englishman in every country), but to an Englishman the word 'foreigner' suggests waiters, hairdressers, organ-grinders and small shopkeepers. The Frenchmen he sees are hairdressers or cooks, the Italians are vendors of ice-cream or plaster images, the Germans used to be waiters, and so on. The Englishman is quite convinced that there are a number of callings for which the foreigner has more aptitude than he has, but they are merely menial callings enjoying a low degree of social prestige. Moreover this is no new development; people have been accustomed in England for centuries to having foreigners round them in menial stations. The foreigner, to them, is a man you pay when you need his services, and the Englishman has a perfectly instinctive feeling of his own superiority, being accustomed to being the master and having the foreigner for his servant. He has recourse to the foreigner for all kinds of services. From Holbein and Van Dyck down to Lazlo, the rulers and nobility of England have had their portraits painted by foreign artists; Italians, and later Germans too, made music for them, while Frenchmen had charge of the refinements of dress and cookery; and Germans, as well as Swiss, were bought for use as soldiers as late as the nineteenth century. Of course no thinking Englishman will take up the point of view that all other people are inferior creatures; but tradition and the habit of centuries will have implanted the feeling of his own superiority in his unconscious mind, making it as hard for him to take an unprejudiced view of a foreigner as it is for the majority of Gentiles to take an unprejudiced view of a Jew.

Having established the fact that the reverse side of English toleration is the consciousness of foreignness, one must bear in mind that the principle of Equality is in general and in every sphere foreign and antagonistic to the Englishman. Equality is a demand of rationalism and logical thought, to which the Englishman, with his individualistic perception of differences and readiness to emphasize and accentuate them, is a stranger. The English idea, even if certainly not always English practice, is the untrammelled development of the individual. Men, animals, plants, objects differ both in kind and individually ; each is perfect when it has completely unfolded the characteristics of its kind and brought its own peculiarities to the highest pitch of development, while every attempt to appear, every desire to become some thing other than what is prescribed by its original nature, is contemptible and unnatural. The principle of English cookery is to let each thing taste of itself and never to cover it up by means of sauces or elaborate ways of preparing it ; and English stuff or a piece of English furniture gets its effect by the goodness of the material, not by added decoration ; English gardening avoids geometry and seeks rather to produce fine individual specimens of trees and plants ; in short, complete development of the individual character is the Englishman's fundamental principle. It is from this angle that he judges human beings also, from which it obviously follows that foreigners are always, and always remain, foreigners ; for it is just as impossible that a Frenchman or a German, to say nothing of more remote nations, should ever become an Englishman as it is that an oak should turn into a beech, beef into venison or a fox-terrier into a bulldog. Conversely, the foreigner wins most respect from the Englishman by showing the most strongly marked peculiarities, by being a perfect specimen in the way that is natural to him.

This attitude is fundamentally different from that of the continental nations, but it is the foundation of the British Empire and the indispensable condition of its existence. The Germans, the French, the Italians, the Spaniards are all 'unitarians,' expecting the foreigner who settles among them to conform to the national pattern; and if he completely adapts himself to their ways of looking at things and prefers their type to his own, he may become one of them and cease to be a foreigner. All the inhabitants of the country have got to have the same culture, talk the same language and, were it possible, belong to the same race: in this way grow up national states with a homogeneous character which are bound to fight the neighbouring culture in their frontier districts, with greater or less success; but great Empires cannot be erected on this principle, however large a territory a national state may have. Among the subjects of the British Empire those of white race do not number so much as one tenth, while the number of Englishmen properly speaking is much smaller still, quite as small as the proportion of Romans among the subjects of the Roman Empire. The great majority of British subjects are foreigners, which is alone enough to make the English attitude towards foreigners necessarily different from the continental. Many of these foreigners enjoy complete equality of rights, still more a partial equality, large numbers are frankly in a position of inferiority; none of them are English, and it never occurs to the Englishman to try to anglicize them. He is himself convinced of the superiority of his own kind, but only as far as he himself is concerned. It has always been part of the English system of government to interfere as little as possible in the subject nations' business and to leave their social and religious customs and habits as far as possible undisturbed: where people adopt English ways they do so at the bidding of taste and conviction, just as a great part of the Continent has done, but the Englishman actually does not like it; on the contrary, one often hears him say that he prefers the native who has remained true to type. He has no interest in all the manifold variety of type, in the population of his Empire and is only too glad to let them be happy after their own fashions as long as they do not disturb him and his friends. Being convinced that they could never become Englishmen, he does not at all want to encourage them in that direction ; he feels that they are foreigners, but it does not occur to him to blame them for their foreignness, which is a fact of nature.

Nothing is more characteristic in this respect than the English attitude to the Jews. In some countries the Jews are attacked as aliens ; in others, less numerous, no distinction is made between them and the rest of the population ; England belongs to neither class. There the Jew is not an Englishman professing the Jewish Faith, still less a man of alien race standing outside the community ; he is simply a Jew who is a British subject and a member of the British Empire, as Australians or Indians, white, yellow and black men, Mohammedans, Catholics and Buddhists are. In this conglomeration of many colours he belongs to one of the minor divisions of the ruling white race ; there is no particular difficulty about fitting him in, no 'Jewish Problem.' Of course there are big differences here too: the East-End Russian Jew who can hardly speak even the most broken English is as much a foreigner in English eyes as any Italian or Pole, while the English Jew whose forbears have been in the country for many generations is as near to him as any other British subject of white race who is not an Englishman. But to maintain that Jews and Englishmen are identical would strike an Englishman as grotesque ; they differ just as the various species of animals and plants differ.

The recognition of this fact does not in itself contain any element of prejudice, but the Englishman would be a superman if he did not prefer his own breed to any other. Beyond that, he is impersonal enough to recognize ability where he finds it and intelligent enough to turn it to good account for the benefit of his country. Since Disraeli's time Jews have frequently filled the highest offices that the British Empire has to bestow, e.g. that of Lord Chief Justice, Viceroy of India and so on ; there are several of them in the Peerage and consequently in Society ; in short, they have exactly the same privileges and chances open to them as any Englishman, but they can no more become Englishmen than a bird can become a fish. It is characteristic of England that the majority of the great Jewish families in it lay stress on their Jewishness and, in many cases, are even orthodox in their practice ; by so doing they win greater respect. It is certainly no unusual thing for Jews to change their names and be baptized, but this happens most frequently among those Jews who have not been in the country long and are accustomed to continental conditions. We must not entirely lose sight of the fact that religious grounds have also had something to do with the favourable position of the Jews in England ; Christianity and the Bible are still a great power there, everybody is familiar with the Old Testament, and biblical Christian names are common ; and the Jews are the people of the Bible. The Englishman's deep reverence for everything ancient with a long tradition behind it comes in here too. 'There were gentlemen among the Jews at a time when our ancestors were still living in caves' said an English schoolmaster to a schoolboy who had said something nasty about Jews in the School.' These sentiments have a very strong hold on the English and have done much to prevent the rise of an anti-semitic movement, which has often seemed imminent in recent years : quite apart from the hatred engendered here as in all countries by the phenomena of disintegration which were attributed to capitalism and thus largely to the Jews, the War made the position of all the large number of Jews with German names very unpleasant, just as the post-War period has done for those with Russian names in consequence of the Bolshevist movement ; but instinct and sentiment have prevented the outbreak of an anti-semitic campaign. The Englishman comes to terms with the complex nature and ambiguous position of the Jews because they are facts ; they are part of the Nature of Things, and the attempt to do violence to nature is contrary to the whole English character.

XI

ART IN ENGLAND

THE English have the reputation of being inartistic;
not only is this the opinion of the outside world, but
even many Englishmen themselves are convinced that
their nation is lacking in artistic instinct. The fact that
England has for many centuries been importing works
of art and artists seems to prove the truth of this view,
but it is, all the same, not quite so easy to decide which
is the cause and which the effect—whether the importation resulted from the absence of home produce or
whether the home country was unable to compete owing
to the importation. To begin with, it is an absurdity
to deny the artistic sense of a whole great nation at one
sweep, though no doubt there are some nations whose
most essential achievements have lain in the domain of
art and others whose artistic achievements are secondary.
Holland is respected and renowned in the world as the
country of Rembrandt and other great painters: certainly no one would describe England as the country of
Reynolds or Turner, but that does not alter the fact
that England has great achievements to her credit in
the domain of art. The stimulus often came from
abroad—indeed the history of European art is full of
examples of the reciprocal influence of the nations on
each other—but in England it always produced something new and unlike anything else. The strong
individualism of the Englishman has seldom allowed of
the foundation of a 'school.' The tradition does not

get carefully preserved and handed down as it does in France ; each individual of genius starts 'scratch' and teaches himself or takes lessons abroad. Incidentally, things are much the same in Germany.

The English school of miniaturists, which is none too well known, produced first-rate work, as a visit to the British Museum will convincingly show ; indeed, English art can, in general, only be seen in England, because the prosperity and undisturbed development of the country have kept a stream of art treasures constantly flowing in but not out. England is incredibly rich in art treasures and even the ever-increasing volume of sales to America is comparatively insignificant. In the Gothic period and at the Renaissance too, English embroidery was highly celebrated. Thus, pretty much at the beginning of what may properly be called English history, painting was in a flourishing condition in England and had reached the same level as in the most important continental countries ; which makes it all the more remarkable that it never developed any further. For centuries afterwards there is no English painting of importance at all. Neither the 'primitive' nor the Renaissance painters of England seem ever to have got beyond the stage of craftsmanship, and Renaissance England imported its art: Henry VII's tomb was built by Torrigiani, and Henry VIII fetched Holbein over. It was not till the eighteenth century that painting in England suddenly blossomed out into a short but glorious prime. The English portrait- and landscape-painters—those are the chief departments of English art—are certainly unthinkable apart from Italian and Dutch influence, but there is just as certainly something absolutely original in their creations ; whatever the value one sets on this art, the peculiar character of its productions unquestionably strikes the eye at once. Their position is very peculiar: the attitude of the experts in all countries towards them is thoroughly condescending, except as regards one or two artists; but the collectors, whose opinion is otherwise chiefly formed under the influence of the experts, pay the most absurd prices for these pictures. Neither the commercial value of an artist's work, however, nor the reputation he enjoys among connoisseurs is constant, and there is no such thing as an absolutely objective judgment in matters of art.

Very little is gained by comparing the work of one school or country with that of another, by comparing Egyptian sculpture with Greek or Gothic art with eighteenth-century art. Painting in Europe has ministered to three Mæcenases, giving expression to their respective ideals—the Church, the courts of princes and *bourgeois* society. English art belongs to the epoch of the last-named and displays its good and bad points, in which respect it bears the most resemblance to Dutch art, which similarly ministered to *bourgeois* society. *Bourgeois* is certainly a very vague concept and open to the objection that English art ministered to the aristocracy, but that would be a purely verbal dispute; the question is not whether a particular portrait represents a noble lady or a middle-class merchant but what the spirit of it is: English art is *bourgeois* because it is not 'heroic' and has nothing of the Grand Style about it, because it has nothing to do with the deeds of Heroes, triumphal processions or allegorical deities, but confines itself to representing human beings. Further, it is not an art of the *salon* either, as French eighteenth-century art, apart from Chardin and Latour, is. It is an art of the park. Its preference for setting its figures in a park for background corresponds to its position half-way between the *salon* and nature, in an environment where much art contrives to produce a natural effect. The portraits of Reynolds, Gainsborough and their lesser followers breathe the same spirit as English gardens of the period, which means that they are a highly cultivated cross between art and nature and at the same time points to their limitations. One does not expect Himalayan peaks or look for tropic glow in an English garden; it can only achieve perfection in its own kind, which, as it appears in these portraits, is graceful yet healthy, simple and with no nonsense about it. The sitters are not flattered or reduced to conventional types, as in Nattier's portraits for instance, and many of them are thoroughly ugly—one has only to think of Reynolds's portraits of Dr. Johnson and Napier, and Raeburn's portraits—yet they all have poise, which is just what many rebels in art cannot forgive them, calling it not Poise but Pose; yet the fact remains that one comes across this same poise everywhere among the same classes in England to-day. It is a matter of tradition and long inheritance, and even a 'naturalist' could not portray these people otherwise; Mr. Chesterton looks a successor of Dr. Johnson, as Lady Diana Cooper does of Lady Hamilton. A dislike for this type of person may make these pictures dislikable, but that, so far from having the smallest connection with their value as works of art, is just as absurd as the contempt of the *Roi Soleil* for the 'vulgarity' of Dutch painting.

That there were even then artists in England whose ideals lay in another direction is proved by Hogarth and Rowlandson, two of the greatest names in English art. The rest may make one think of parks, but they make one think of the East End and Bank Holidays: they are anti-puritanical, for all the moral exhortations in Hogarth's series, hard-hitting, popular in tone and full of humour—in short, as much Saxon as the Reynoldses and Gainsboroughs are Norman.

Landscape-painting flourished alongside of portraiture. The Dutch influence stands to reason here, Holland being the cradle of all landscape-painting, added to which there is the similarity between the two countries in their damp maritime climate, the preponderance of grey cloudy skies, and the greenness of the landscape. But with Constable English painting emancipated itself from all models and in Turner it gained an artist of unique genius. There are no standards for appraising this painter of light; one has to accept him completely or pass him completely by. In my opinion his fame would be infinitely greater if his works had ever been visible outside England; to the vast majority of people he is only known in reproductions, which cannot convey the slightest idea of the character of his work. Undoubtedly, as Claude Monet among others has testified, he was the stimulus that produced impressionistic landscape-painting and the father of the great movement which dominated a whole generation of European painters. Landscape-painting provides a good example of the interaction of the arts of different nations; the movement goes from Holland to England, thence through Constable to France, where it produced the school of Fontainebleau which in its turn influenced Holland; in the same way Turner influenced the Impressionists and they Germany. It is the first time in the history of English painting that it exercises influence instead of undergoing it, which is all the more reason for appreciating the significance of this fact.

This great period was followed by a very minor one. The only movement of any interest in English art during the nineteenth century is the Pre-Raphaelite movement, and the interest of it belongs to craftsmanship and literature rather than to painting. It was William Morris who brought about the renascence of the handicrafts in Europe and re-awakened the feeling for materials and for quality, however far the movement may subsequently have departed from his mediaeval ideals. The Pre-Raphaelites have been the inspiration of a number of poets and musicians, e.g. Maeterlinck and Debussy, who are unthinkable apart from them, and were the stimulus which produced the wave of Symbolism and Æstheticism which came to the Continent from England, as Aubrey Beardsley stimulated the growth of a new style of drawing, and Oscar Wilde, through his *Salome*, a new orientalism—both of them, incidentally, being far more highly prized on the Continent than in England. The Pre-Raphaelites were thus an important factor in the development of European art; there is only one thing that they were definitely not, and that is, important painters. They did great damage to English painting in directing it into wholly literary channels; this danger is anyhow never far away in England, because the feeling for the 'story' in a picture ('every little picture tells a story') and its 'message' comes much more naturally to the Englishman than the feeling for its pictorial value: hence the extremely low artistic level of the average picture.

Since the Pre-Raphaelites there has been no more English painting, even if there have been one or two painters of importance, like Whistler, Sargent and Augustus John. There are a number of excellent painters in England to-day, but they are European painters, deriving, like those of every other country, from Paris—from Cézanne, Matisse and Picasso.

In the domain of sculpture England has never produced first-rate work. The greater part of the sculpture in the cathedrals was destroyed by the Puritans, but the surviving examples suggest the conclusion that this art never reached the continental level in England. Here, too, the similarity to Holland is notable, and it is probably the climate that is responsible for the deficiency; mists and blurred outlines do not go well with sculpture, and this same atmosphere is very likely the reason why English architecture goes for pronouncedly picturesque effects. Simple, clear, geometrical shapes and big unbroken surfaces can be enlivened by the play of sunlight and shadow, but in a hazy light they are ineffective and frigid. The ordinary simple house of the South, without any pretensions to architectural merit, is a cube with smooth walls and a flat, or at any rate low, roof; the corresponding house in England has projecting bits and gables, dark timbers set off against light stonework, and every kind of variety of window, chimney and ground-plan.

Architecturally England is one of the richest countries of Europe, and the greatness of the work that she has produced in this sphere from the earliest times is alone sufficient to demolish the ridiculous notion that the Englishman is no artist. It stands to reason that English architecture has, like that of every country, been influenced from abroad, but it is one of the richest in content and most original in Europe. Its strength lies in imagination, instinct for the picturesque and sense of effect, but above all, in its feeling for the symphony of nature and building, and in these respects it is unequalled and a model to the world; on the other hand it lacks the Latin sense of proportion and harmony, Latin logic in fact, because they are contrary to the deepest instincts of the Englishman's soul.

The Romanesque style came into England with the Normans, and the 'Saxon' style that had prevailed till then only remained in minor buildings, but the

Norman buildings in England had a character of their own from the first. The Norman cathedrals of England are heavier and more massive, longer and lower than those of Northern France, with heavy square towers. In almost every case the building of the cathedral took such a time that Gothic bits got added, and some of the most magnificent, e.g. Durham, Winchester, Ely and Peterborough, are in this mixed style. The ground-plan generally shows a rectangular end (the curve being out of harmony with the English character, a fact from which psycho-analysts may draw far-reaching conclusions) with a further extension in the shape of an equally rectangular chapel: the picturesqueness of the outline is heightened by towers, the centre tower generally being the chief one; which forms the characteristic silhouette of an English cathedral. In almost all cases the cathedral is surrounded by a number of ecclesiastical buildings—chapels, cloisters, chapter-house, houses of the clergy or monastic buildings—which generally combine to make up one great whole in a setting of gardens and trees, forming an architectural group of unequalled charm.

The Renaissance gave England the Tudor style, perhaps the most English of them all. It has a bad name among the specialists because it cheerfully mixes up Gothic and Renaissance features and puts in products of its own fancy as well. It builds its country houses on an E-shaped plan in honour of Queen Elizabeth, puts Gothic battlements on top of walls with pilasters, ornaments its roofs with a forest of elaborate chimneys, uses red tiles, stone and timber all mixed up together, in short, does pretty well everything that is contrary to the rules and prohibited. Could one not say just the same about another product of this period, the work of Shakespear? This English Renaissance is equally lawless, full-blooded and 'romantic' in all its manifestations. The Tudor period produced the loveliest country seats of England; it invented the country house that had ceased to be a castle and become a house set informally in its natural surroundings and growing together with them into a unity—a thoroughly and exclusively English conception. On the other hand the town houses of the period, which survive in considerable numbers in towns like York, Chester and Tewkesbury, as also its delightful cottages, bear a far greater resemblance to those of the Continent. It was a secular age which built few churches; but, as against that, it saw the foundation of most of the Oxford and Cambridge Colleges, which are every bit as purely English productions as the country houses. The typical college, which came into existence as a place of clerical education, is built round a big quadrangle entered from the street by a towered gateway; chapel, dining-hall and rooms, fused together into a unity, surround the green lawn which adorns the central court; new quadrangles, each enclosed in itself, were added as the colleges grew. In Oxford and Cambridge these groups of buildings abut on one another, the continuity being interrupted by churches, libraries and the Schools of the University; both towns are real architectural museums and, considered as a whole, the most worth seeing, perhaps, of all England's artistic achievements and one of the greatest of Europe's.

In the seventeenth century the classicism of Palladio came in, but England had practically no baroque period, in the continental sense, in architecture, though it did in handicrafts and furniture; and very soon afterwards a strong Dutch influence came over with William of Orange. The great architect of the period is Wren, whose masterpiece, St. Paul's Cathedral, is a very perfect piece of work which would be equally in place in any other country; but the towers of his churches, of which he entirely re-built sixty in the City alone after the Great Fire, are full of fancifulness and indigenous Gothic romanticism. Dutch influence affected gardening and the town house, while the town got rid of its fortifications and acquired more space; this led to the growth of the self-contained house, which is as characteristic of England as it is of Holland. Houses got smaller and lower and a narrow two- or three-storied detached house, with a simple front and a garden behind, became the standard; decoration was used extremely sparingly, the door alone being somewhat more richly ornamented in most cases. Houses like this are conceived as members of a row forming a unity. In this period England invented the square, a quadrangular space bounded by houses which have been built as a homogeneous architectural unity, while the space in the middle is occupied by a large garden which belongs to the inhabitants of the houses in common. London still has a large number of lovely squares, mostly dating from the end of the eighteenth century or the beginning of the nineteenth. English urban architecture, from its exemplary excellence in this period, proceeded to sink lower and lower as the nineteenth century went on, in common with the architecture of the whole of Europe. The builders of country houses alone did good work in every age. The town houses of this period are not so bad; the type which had already been erected was preserved, only the houses are clumsier, not nearly so well-proportioned, and built of stucco instead of honest brick. The public and 'show' buildings of the period—with a few exceptions mostly belonging to the Gothic Revival, like the Houses of Parliament and the Law Courts—are no better and no worse than those on the Continent: some are conventional without being positively unpleasant, others intolerably ostentatious and spurious, like the contemporary buildings in Berlin. It is the commercial and office buildings, where this ready-made finery is particularly out of place, that are, alas, particularly hard to shut one's eyes to ; nor is the mass production of the cheaper suburbs among the most cheering phenomena.

Since the end of the War an extraordinary fit of building has come over London, and no other city has altered its appearance so thoroughly. There has been good, bad and indifferent work. Regent Street, which has been entirely re-built, must be the only case of a main street built on a definite plan for a long time. It is a pity that it has not turned out better than it has, and it is easy to criticize it on the ground of ill-conceived ornamentation and other mistakes ; but when all's said and done, here is a main street deliberately planned and built as a whole and uniform in material and proportions, whereas in Berlin and Paris (e.g. the Boulevard Raspail or the Boulevard Haussmann) anyone who wants to build is allowed to go ahead at his own sweet will without any general plan. The great thoroughfare of Kingsway similarly shows that it has been conceived as a unity, and, far as both streets are from perfection, I can think of nothing in Europe at the present day to compare with them. Some of the monster office buildings, such as Adelaide House, Bush House etc., are excellent ; equally excellent buildings and in infinitely greater quantities are, however, to be seen in the towns of America and, in lesser quantities, in those of Germany. This style, which is prosaic and logical realism raised to monumental power, has spread over the whole world from America and Germany where it started ; but there is just one characteristic difference in the attitude of the nations to it that is worth noting : America is proud of her sky-scrapers, Germany admires her Chile-haus in Hamburg and her Bauhaus in Dessau, but England, apart from professionals and small artistic circles, thinks this new architecture horrible. Chesterton has protested against the attempt to turn London into a 'second-rate New York,' and the average Englishman, so far as he cares about the question at all, dislikes these new buildings: they are un-English. Here is one of the many points at which the deep-rooted individualism of the English comes into collision with the spirit of the age of machinery and technology; perhaps England will will find a private solution of her own for this problem too, but it is difficult to foresee one, because the same needs force people to the same solutions: just as motor cars and underground railways and steamships are the same all over the world, so has this business architecture become a standardized product. At any rate there is a universally applicable new architectural style, at least for all utility buildings.

The Englishman himself is the first to admit that art plays no great part in his country and is treated in stepmotherly fashion; no wonder the rest of the world repeats and believes it; but all the same, the case is not so simple. The truth is that for the last hundred years art has in fact played a very minor part in every country: people ostensibly attach a very high value to it, but they bother very little about it, and a thousand times more importance attaches to commerce and industry everywhere. The position of art is relatively strongest in France; but where do artists occupy a position of real importance in the State to-day? What parliament or what government is susceptible to the influence of the art-world as it is to the influence of finance and industry? Art has been a minor thing in national life everywhere for a long time; in England they are more honest about it—that seems to me to be the chief difference. The objection that the State does not subsidize art (the opera, theatre etc.) in England as it does in other countries will not hold water. The fact is that the State leaves a great deal to private enterprise in England because that is part of the English character ; neither the hospitals nor the railways, neither the principal universities nor the Stock Exchange are maintained or supervised by the State. In every country art is a matter of interest to a certain portion of Polite Society, a portion, that is, of the *bourgeoisie*. I am prepared to believe that this class is smaller in England than, say, in Germany, but I do not much believe in the genuineness of its enthusiasm for art anywhere: in the lean years it disappeared like greased lightning everywhere, and the position of artists is certainly no worse in England than in other countries.

The average Englishman does not rate art particularly highly. He does not go as far as Plato, who, as is well known, saw no use for artists at all in his ideal state ; but he only has a use for the art and the artists who fit into the social life of the nation and minister to definite needs. He wants to have good portraits and a certain number of sound pictures on the walls of his rooms— i.e. he wants exactly the same thing as the Amsterdam or Haarlem burgher wanted in his day. He has little appreciation of experiments in pure art and his taste is conservative: for the painters who conform to it he has official Honours, and members of the Royal Academy enjoy a high social position and command good prices; all the rest are left to the care of the few knowledgeable people of taste who buy 'modern' pictures. The number of these is, I believe, no smaller in England than on the Continent ; for there are a great many young painters in England who live by their work : all I do believe is that there are far fewer people in England who profess to be art lovers and have got a lot of names by heart for fear of being written down as uncultured.

This fear, which is a special mark of the real *petit bourgeois*, is unknown to the Englishman, who is not in the least afraid of making a fool of himself on this point and has kept his attitude of simple-minded cheerful incomprehension towards matters of art intact ; for there is no intellectual snobbery about him. On the other hand he is an artist in things in which he has no idea that 'art' is involved at all. This fatal cleavage between Fine Art—i.e. easel pictures and statues— and house-furnishing, handicrafts, clothes, and daily life in fact, is the most grievous legacy of the nineteenth century. The Englishman is an artist in houses, gardens and clothes ; nowhere are there so many beautiful houses and so much unerring taste in the furnishing of them as in England, which has a very ancient tradition of domestic life and is in fact the creator of the modern house. The dining-room came from England—Versailles had nothing but *salons*, some of which contained beds of state, while meals were served in others ; the bedroom, the billiard-room, the hall, the library, bathrooms and lavatories were all evolved in England, which also created the country house and the hotel, the successor of the inn ; and since the days of Chippendale and Sheraton it has made the best furniture, as it does the finest silver, the best leather goods and the best cloth.

The Englishman is quite unaware of the existence of an art of the home, but it is comparatively difficult for him to furnish in bad taste, because the things he finds in the shops are mostly good. It is not at all his idea to imitate the *salons* of a palace ; his drawing-room has comfortable sofas and chairs in it. It never even occurs to him that he invented the 'club' arm-chair; all he did was to buy comfortable things to sit on. He knows when the wood is good and the cover looks decent, but he has no notion that that is Modern Interior Decoration. For centuries he has been piling up art treasures of every kind—furniture, Chinese porcelain, Persian carpets, Italian and Dutch pictures—and thus his taste has gradually been formed and become instinctive. He would laugh if you told him that his flower-beds and table-decorations prove that he has the instincts of an artist, and if you tried to maintain, what is very true, that the tweed of his suits, the silk of his ties and the linen of his shirts are artistic, as is likewise the way he combines them (in which matter it is remarkable how far ahead the male half of the English nation is in knowledgeableness and taste), he would assume that you were making fun of him or that you had a screw slightly loose. One may therefore say in conclusion that art in the true sense of the word has got so thoroughly into the bones of large sections of the English people (or better, remained there, since it was common property everywhere as late as the eighteenth century) that it is no longer recognized as such, because people have got into the habit of confining the category of 'art' in their minds to pictures and sculptures. Towards art in that sense the average Englishman's attitude shows no great understanding; it is definitely not a necessity of life to him. And let any nation that can maintain that the majority of itself is constituted differently cast the first stone.

XII

ENGLISH LITERATURE

Not merely in Latin countries but in Germany too there is a tendency to regard the English as business people lacking the artistic instinct of the continental nations; Napoleon's remark about the 'nation of shopkeepers' has gained only too much credence. Over against that there is the fact that England has in the course of many centuries produced a literature which that of no other country is in a class to touch for richness and many-sidedness; this 'prosaic,' 'unimaginative' nation has given birth to the greatest poets and created the most important drama. It seems as if England had concentrated her whole artistic activity on words; her music is insignificant, her sculpture does not count, her painting is not in the first rank, but the richness of her literature is unsurpassed.

The legends of England are of Celtic origin, the sagas of the Arthurian cycle (Tristan etc.) coming from Cornwall and Brittany, which is racially akin to it; and we may safely attribute great importance, as regards the creative power of the English, to the Celtic strain in their blood: the long-accomplished fusion of the component races naturally makes it impossible to prove this, but the frequency of Irish, and to a lesser degree of Scottish, descent among the English poets also points in the same direction. Certain it is that in the first great flowering-time of English literature, the Elizabethan age, superabundance of imagination and emotion was already its most essential feature, and they are qualities that do not seem to fit in with the English character as other nations imagine it.

The dramatists of this period, which culminates in Shakespear, created the modern drama—the third, following on the ancient drama and the drama of the Church, that Europe has produced. England created the modern theatre. The works of Shakespear no doubt belong to humanity in general, but they are in the first place exceedingly English, a fact that people in other countries where they flatter themselves that they appreciate Shakespear quite as well as people in England do, if not better, are reluctant to admit. Shakespear is the grand individualist, the creator of individuals not types: which is the greater accomplishment is debatable. His characters are open to many interpretations, eccentric, often grotesque; a true English 'spleen' appears in Hamlet, a true English humour in his clowns.

Shakespearean tragedy is not unalloyed pathos, it is shot through with grotesque features: thus Hamlet is flabby, Othello is a black man, Shylock oscillates between horror and grotesque comedy. Conversely, Shakespearean comedy is often full of melancholy and horror. Shakespear's characters are like the English—misty, without sharp outlines, pointing not in one but in many directions, and any one of them admits of a whole host of interpretations. His female characters are thoroughly English girls too: Desdemona, Cordelia, Ophelia belong to the type of the fair-haired girl, half child, that is still the English ideal of womenhood; more subtle, perhaps, are the girls in his comedies, the Rosalinds and Violas who come on dressed as boys, the English female type that has the world at its feet to-day. With Lady Macbeth and Cleopatra he also created the second Anglo-Saxon stage and cinema type, namely, the Vamp.

The Shakespearean clown who appears in so many variant forms is perhaps the most typically English : in his finest creations, from the bumpkins in *A Midsummer-Night's Dream* and the grave-diggers in *Hamlet* down to the melancholy Jaques in *As You Like It*, Shakespear ranges over the whole gamut of gradations between the coarsest jesting and the most profound humour passing into Tragedy—between Pantaloon and Charlie Chaplin, the best existing representative of the Shakespearean spirit. As Jaques symbolizes the 'splenetic' Englishman, so does Falstaff the John-Bull kind. All Shakespear's characters are exceedingly English, even if they transcend such limits and become simply human.

One can also get a clear idea how English the spirit of Shakespear was by the opposite procedure, i.e. by thinking of the types he did not create, which were developed by other races. There is no Don Juan and no Manon or Carmen in Shakespear, i.e. no one whose tragedy is conditioned by their sex-lives; nor is there a Faust, whose tragedy lies in his craving for knowledge. Those are un-English types, as un-English as the characters of traditional classical drama, intensified on a single side, of which those of the French dramatists are the most typical. In Shakespear there is no purely heroic hero like the Cid, no *Avare* who is just Avarice incarnate—compare the complexity of Shylock with Molière's character. Unity of meaning is a product of clearer skies and sharper contours; classical drama always reminds one of sculpture, that most genuine Southern art ; the drama of Shakespear approximates to painting and music, which are at the other end of the scale of modes of artistic expression. The life of the woods, flowers and trees, rain, storm and thunder and cloud and the sound of the sea are in his work: without the English climate and English scenery he is inconceivable, and it is precisely the highest summits of his achievement, *King Lear*, *Macbeth* and *The Tempest*, that contain the grandest English landscape painting. Shakespear is lawless, illogical, contingent as Nature herself, and it is this instinctive quality that is the really English thing about him. A Shakespear play is the result of growth in defiance of all classical rules, just exactly as London and the British Empire are. Any student of Aristotle can convict Shakespear of a thousand faults of construction, just as any architect could design a more sensible plan for a town and any continental constitutional lawyer draw up a more logical constitution; but this city, this Empire and these dramas, with all their faults and all their overwhelming greatness, could, in their careless freedom, only have been the work of Englishmen.

The modern novel, as well as modern drama, is an English creation. The novel is pre-eminently the *bourgeois* art-form, and it is by no accident that its ancestor, *Don Quixote*, is the great satire on the heroic. The development was from sagas of the Gods by way of the heroic epic to aristocratic drama, into which the eighteenth century for the first time introduced middle-class people as comic figures: *bourgeois* tragedy was not to come till the nineteenth century, but the *bourgeois* makes his first appearance as chief character or 'hero' in the English novel as early as the eighteenth. This period saw the discovery of the ordinary man and every-day life and of the appropriate form for describing them, namely prose narrative. The hero of one of the most celebrated novels of the period is called, like the book itself, Tom Jones, which signifies the discovery that people of inferior social rank are just as interesting and worth writing about as princes and dukes. This seems obvious to-day, but at the time it was an unheard-of audacity, an audacity but for which the whole of European fiction would now be non-existent. The English novel developed side by side with English democracy, from which it cannot be separated; the two things go together like French classical drama and the Court of Versailles. Fielding, Smollett and Goldsmith, who influenced the German novel through Goethe, are the ancestors of all representation of *bourgeois* careers and *bourgeois* life. Sterne with his *Tristram Shandy* is the father of prose humorists, Swift with his *Gulliver's Travels* of the social satire. It was Holland, not England, that had the first *bourgeois* culture in the modern sense and developed the *bourgeois* painting which England subsequently took over; but England gave modern culture its first literary expression.

These may be the two most important epochs in English literature, but they are by no means isolated. Before the Renaissance period Chaucer had already done great work, and after it generation after generation of great writers followed in almost unbroken succession. In the reciprocal relations between English and continental literature England has nearly always been the giving party. Between Shakespear and the eighteenth century lies the period of Restoration drama, which has just in the last few years returned to great popularity, while it has remained, strange to say, unknown in other countries. The Restoration period, when the Stuarts were reinstated after the Puritan movement had run its course, is full of a cheerful and pretty coarse joy in life, which the drama of the period, chiefly social comedy, reflects; notions of morality have become elastic, with virtue nowhere and wit and repartee at a premium. In actual dramatic quality these plays are weak, but the dialogue is often brilliant. The comedies of Wilde and many of the drawing-room plays of to-day are descendants of Restoration drama.

Far as it is from the greatness of the Shakespearean epoch, this movement is nevertheless thoroughly worthy of attention as the second golden age of English drama.

Another interesting thing is the hostility of the spirit of Puritanism towards the drama and the theatre, the consequence of which is that when Puritanism is on top, drama decays while the novel flourishes, but in the periods in which the aristocratic and pleasure-loving side of the English character gets on top, the drama revives with it. In England Puritanism (i.e. extreme Protestantism) goes with democracy, the *bourgeois* spirit and prose narrative, as Catholicism (or the High Church) does with aristocracy, the feudal spirit and the drama—that is, the peasant and *bourgeois* Saxon elements over against the chivalric and aristocratic Norman and Celtic elements. The age of Elizabeth is dramatic and aristocratic, that of the Puritans democratic, with Milton for its great poet and a religious epic; the Restoration reinstated the nobility and the drama in their rights, but the middle classes and the novel came to the top under the Protestant and prosaic William of Orange. With the Romantic movement, of which England is the chief starting point, the pendulum swings back to the chivalric and aristocratic, its greatest poet being Byron, a dramatist: it instinctively harks back to the Norman mediaeval tradition, at the same time receiving a strong stimulus from the Celtic side (e.g. Ossian and Scott). The result was a new efflorescence of English poetry, dramatic and lyric, and of the historical novel, with Byron, Scott, Shelley and Keats. The Victorian age marks a return, which gathers strength as it advances, to middle-class Puritanism and democracy. In it begins, with Dickens and Thackeray, the second golden age of the novel, which has both the strong and the weak points of Puritan *bourgeois* England, its solid comfortable *gemütlichkeit* (a German notion, but is there a more homely writer than Dickens?) and its sound and humorous sobriety, but also its tendency to moralize, which everyone who is not an Anglo-Saxon finds unbearable. The Drama sank lower and lower.

The later Victorian age produced two prose writers who are perhaps the greatest England has had and are properly appreciated neither at home nor abroad, where they are practically unknown—Meredith and Thomas Hardy. Meredith, one of the most subtle psychologists of all time, suffers from the excessive richness of his fancy: limiting himself to the depiction of the upper classes, he eliminates everything of a merely material interest and confines himself to tracking down the characters of his personages into their minutest ramifications, in which process the superabundance of associations, ingenious conceits and digressions gets in the way of the management and development of his theme; but certain single characters of his, like the Egoist, Diana of the Crossways or Richard Feverel, are among the few immortal figures of European fiction. Thomas Hardy is the great epic poet in prose; his village tragedies, *Tess of the d'Urbervilles, The Mayor of Casterbridge* etc., in their uncompromising fatalism, have the grandeur of the ancients. Meredith was too 'obscure' in his day, Hardy too 'pessimistic.' The tremendous broadening out and levelling down of literature began in England, as it did elsewhere, about the middle of the nineteenth century: cheap daily papers, cheap periodicals, in every sense cheap novels were the concomitants of the universal extension of 'education'; the entire nation began to read, but it demanded literature to suit its tastes. This problem may be the same in every country, but it arises in a particularly well-defined form in England, the difference in education and real culture between classes being much greater there than on the Continent. The intellectual aristocracy, like the social, is small in numbers, though it ranks very high ; hence the best writers are seldom popular, or in any case have great difficulty in establishing themselves, while indescribably insipid stuff which panders to the taste of the multitude enjoys huge sales—a phenomenon not altogether unknown in the country of Frau Courts-Mahler too. While Hardy and Meredith were establishing themselves with the greatest difficulty, Hall Caine, Marie Corelli and such people were enjoying unheard-of triumphs ; Browning and Swinburne were unpopular, while *The Idylls of the King* was considered great poetry.

It was near the end of the century before things began to take a turn for the better, undoubtedly in consequence of the spiritual emancipation of large sections of the middle classes, and England had another literary revival. We are still too near it to-day to recognize its greatness—nearly all its most important representatives are still alive—but I do not hesitate to affirm that this 'Pre-War Generation' (to give it a collective name which clearly distinguishes it from the present one) is the most important in English literature since the age of Elizabeth. During the reigns of the two queens, Elizabeth and Victoria, political power and cultural achievement both reached a climax together. Kipling, Wells, Conrad, Chesterton, Shaw, Galsworthy were, and except Conrad still are, all writing at the same time; they have all won deserved fame all over the world, because they all contributed something new. Kipling conquered the reading public in every country with the *Jungle Books* and his Indian novels and short stories, only to lose it again in his later period, which was tinged with imperialism. To-day he is perhaps under-rated through being too closely identified with the period of Jingoism which reached its climax in the Boer War. He reminds one of Joseph Chamberlain, Cecil Rhodes, Lord Northcliffe, and the unscrupulous men of Blood and Iron who controlled English policy at the end of last century; he was the bard of this imperialism whose brutal strength is akin to his own. It is no coincidence that these leading figures of the period, on whose shoulders the Victorian régime went to its last resting-place, were all *parvenus* and wielders of the mailed fist.

In spirit, though not in time, Kipling belongs to a period long dead and buried, earlier than that of Wells, Shaw and Chesterton. Theirs may be called the age of Social Criticism in which the existing order of society was arraigned and condemned: their activity runs parallel with the great Scandinavians and Russians. Wells and Shaw both played an important part in the development of the English Labour Party and their literary works are in many cases primarily controversial. Shaw's dramatic works constitute an assault on the grand scale directed against convention, in which he attacks sham heroism and sham morality, sham sexual ethics and sham Puritanism. And yet he is at bottom a typical Puritan and a typical Protestant: the English middle classes regarded him for years as a terrible revolutionary and iconoclast, but Society always found his eagerness a little comical, because it believes in the underlying truth of the conventions, which serve its purposes, quite as little as Shaw himself does. He is a child of the age of Darwin and Higher Criticism, a rationalist who believes in Evolution, but he is also one of the subtlest and wittiest minds of this century; the problems with which he is concerned will no doubt soon have become as 'unreal' as those of his master, Ibsen, have already, but he will survive as a great satirist, as Ibsen will as a great dramatist: to-day he is the only man writing for the stage who has an international reputation.

Wells is an unusually many-sided writer. His early works were daring fantasies on a scientific foundation, Utopias and visions with an astonishing power of carrying conviction. These were followed by novels with a social bias, like *Kipps*, the life-story of a little insignificant average Englishman, *Tono Bungay*, his delicious satire on the power of publicity, and the rest ; he has a sympathetic understanding of dull, inarticulate, ordinary people who are not particularly good and not particularly wicked, and has feeling where Shaw has wit. His later novels which depict higher classes are less convincing : in this sphere he is surpassed by Galsworthy, whose masterpiece, the *Forsyte Saga*, will remain the classic picture of the English patriciate—as distinct from the aristocracy—as Thomas Mann's *Die Buddenbrocks* is of the German. The thing that he, Wells and Shaw have in common is their conviction of the indefensibility of the social order, their revolutionary tendency. Shaw's great opponent, Chesterton, is every bit as much of a revolutionary, only his revolutionary ideal is diametrically opposed to theirs ; he is a Catholic anti-evolutionary. The originality of the man lies in his championship of a gay enjoyment of life ; he attacks the age for being gloomy, servile and mechanized, without colour and without soul. The reaction he wants to see is a return to the 'merrie England' which has been destroyed by the commercial spirit, industrialism, Protestantism and a pedantic belief in science. He is perhaps even wittier, more brilliant and more full of paradox than Shaw. Shaw, with his ideas of Progress and Freedom, is thin and ascetic, neither drinks nor smokes, and is a vegetarian ; Chesterton, the reactionary Churchman, is a Falstaff—corpulent, sanguine, a keen drinker and a devotee of all the pleasures of life. There is certainly no other country in which the two rival attitudes to life are championed by two such original, fertile and really significant minds. Shaw and Chesterton would alone be enough to stamp their period as one of the great ages of the English genius. Conrad kept entirely away from these problems in his work; perhaps his foreign origin—he was a Pole by birth—had something to do with keeping him off English social questions. His themes are the sailor's life, the South Seas and the countries of the negro races, and in his penetrating psychology he sometimes recalls Dostoevsky; he is also, odd as it may seem, the greatest English stylist of the age.

The above-mentioned are all still active, with the exception of Conrad who died a few years ago, and they will no doubt give to the world further work of high value; but they tell us nothing of the spirit of the present generation of writers. The World War meant a break with the past for English literature too, and the spirit of to-day's generation is different from the spirit of yesterday's. It is easier to characterize it in a negative sort of way than to define it positively, because we are here concerned with a process of development which we have to seize while it is still going on and cannot see in perspective; it is partly the problems that have changed and partly the attitude of writers towards them.

In this context a comparison with Germany is not without interest. There the upheavals of the War and the Revolution led to a demand for 'activism' in literature; the writer was required to give up his preoccupation with the purely æsthetic and 'æsthete' became a term of abuse; it was his bounden duty at least to exert a political influence and help in the solution of social problems through his writings, even if he could not, as people hoped he might in the first confusion of the Revolution, take part in the direction of public affairs himself. In short, what people demanded was literature with a purpose, the very thing that the previous generation regarded as the sin against the Holy Ghost in art. In England just the opposite happened. It was the pre-War generation that had fulfilled the demands just described, the Shaws and the Wellses and the Chestertons being the writers with a purpose and actively political : hence in England the reaction of the younger generation took the form of a movement away from Purpose and a rejection of everything to do with politics.

The younger generation—incidentally a similar development may be expected in Germany—is disillusioned and *blasé*. The upshot of the War, which the simple-minded among the English thought was to be a crusade for democracy and freedom and to create a new world, is impoverishment, class hatred and enslavement. With the foundations of the social structure quaking, Shaw and Wells seem to young people to-day to be flogging dead horses, and after the experience of Russian Bolshevism people no longer look to socialistic reform or the rise of the proletariat to produce the millennium. These ideals have gone into liquidation, as the ideals of 1848 did in the Germany of Bismarck, but, as ideals always do, only for a time ; so far, however, no new ones have been put in their place. England does not exactly hunger and thirst after ideals at the moment ; people have come to recognize only too clearly how hollow and false idealistic phrases are ; they no longer believe in the idea of making mankind happy, least of all do they regard it as the aim and content of literature. The great influence that Russian literature and psychoanalysis have exercised in England works in the same direction. Psychology has acquired a new and profounder outlook and the work of its earlier exponents seems naïve and superficial now : sex and its problems have had their importance recognized as never before ; and there are quite a number of preachers in England who give their congregations sermons on psycho-analysis, whether in its favour or against it. Concurrently with this, the idea of the moral responsibility of the individual for his actions has declined, if it has not altogether dissolved ; and even the concept of the unity of the personality is called in question. Thus all established conceptions—the order of society, moral ideas, the responsibility of the individual—have begun to wobble ; nothing is secure and there is nothing over which one can get excited.

Such is the origin of the outlook of the present generation of writers, which takes the absence of all conviction for granted as a starting point and regards all things as equally important or unimportant. But this *Nitchevo* is not the Russian kind ; the Anglo-Saxon reaction, with certain exceptions which will be discussed later, is something quite different, a humorous one. 'Life is a tale told by an idiot . . . . signifying nothing,' said Shakespear long ago, and not even the most pessimistic of Slavs could put it more incisively ; but Shakespear was far from being a prophet of pessimism, and the writers of the present day are equally far from it. Life is a senseless idiotic business, 'problems' are absurd, political and social questions a bore, progress an illusion, but it does not follow that life is a tragedy—that would also be a sign that one was attaching importance to the unimportant ; it is a farce with tragic bits in it, in fact, in the genuine English view, a clown's show. Norman Douglas, Aldous Huxley, David Garnett, Gerhardi and Osbert Sitwell are among the prophets of this philosophy of life. In *South Wind* Douglas gathers his cosmopolitan company on a southern island, where, the conventions having all been blown away by the South Wind, they make love, cheat and even murder according to the dictates of impulse : it is all of no particular importance but highly amusing, a play from which no moral can be drawn, its amorality being obvious, but a very diverting one, in the way that the habits and customs of ants might be. Huxley's novels are written in the same spirit. They take one to castles or country houses in Italy or England, among people remote from the cares of daily life who tell each other stories or live their own in a half-amused way. His books have something of the tone of the Decameron about them : the people in them are safe, and though they know that outside the plague is raging, they are determined to forget it ; their humour is often grim. David Garnett tell stories, in language of a classic beauty, about women who turn into animals and men who go and live in the monkeys' cage, beautiful, impossible yet convincing fairy tales for highly sophisticated grown-up children. Sitwell laughs at the customs and the morality of pre-War England, sends his whole company flying up into the air and turns the most abominable gossiping old woman of the lot into a national heroine. Gerhardi, who is of Anglo-Russian descent, treats Russian subjects in a spirit of bitter Anglo-Saxon humour : *Futility*, the title of his first novel, might stand as the epitome of this whole school's outlook.

The second main movement of the present-day has the Irishman James Joyce for its most brilliant representative ; in the eyes of his followers he is the greatest genius of the age, and his influence, particularly on American literature, is tremendous. His chief work, *Ulysses*, is a description of any day in the life of any Dubliner, but the senselessness of things is not accepted with a coldly aristocratic gesture and a shrug of the shoulders here ; the book is a wild, despairing, derisive attack on life, written in blood and tears. The hero's thoughts are investigated down to their last and minutest articulations and written down, not in the way that was customary in literature, but brutally and in the raw, with absolutely complete veracity, and packed with all the hidden vulgarity and unbridled appetites which he does not even admit to himself. Joyce is, besides, an artist of the first rank in language, a creator of new possibilities in technique. If one is not prepared to grant him genius one must at least admit his brilliant gifts ; he is undoubtedly the most interesting figure among present-day writers. There are other Irishmen, like O'Flaherty and the dramatist O'Casey, who are equally super-realists in this new sense. English Literature boggles at nothing to-day : where it is not coldly cynical, it attacks everything that once passed under the name of convention and morality with unbounded violence ; in a word, it is anti-Puritan. But when the Anglo-Saxon does attack the Puritan, he is, consciously or unconsciously, attacking the Puritan in himself—which holds good of the Jews and the Germans too. That is just the reason why he loses all moderation : it is impossible for him to be simple, sensuous, pagan and non-moral, like a Latin ; his Paganism is self-conscious. But this same lack of moderation makes possible those individual manifestations of genius in which England is so rich, the Shakespears and Swifts and Turners and Joyces.

English literature of to-day shows no falling off and it is safe to assume that it will continue in the future to carry on the great tradition of many centuries : now as ever there is an astonishing wealth of talent about, and English poetry seems to enjoy an everlasting summer. If one confined one's attention to literary history one could not help regarding England, where every generation has produced great men, as the paradise of poetry, drama and the novel ; but England would not be England if this logical conclusion corresponded to the actual state of affairs. The truth is not so simple. Together with what is perhaps the greatest literature of Europe, England, since the middle of the nineteenth century at least, has also produced the largest and most degraded body of trash in Europe ; it is only quite recently that she has yielded in this sphere too to American competition. Nowhere does one find so many unspeakably silly novels, such cheap lyrics or plays aimed so shamelessly at the gallery. It is not merely that the work of literary value constitutes only a small fraction of the total literary production—one is accustomed to take that for granted ; but, in addition to that, these relatively few exceptions for the most part have but small success with the public. For several generations the best writers have been unpopular and the popular writers insignificant. Blake, Swinburne and Browning enjoyed a limited popularity, and the public preferred Hall Caine, Marie Corelli and Ouida to Hardy and Meredith, and Pinero to Bernard Shaw. Things are just the same to-day : most of the writers I have discussed are hardly known to the great public, and the most important of them, Joyce, is not generally read for the simple reason that his chief work is banned by the censor in England, as also in the United States.

Though England is full of talent, the general level is exceedingly low, which looks like a paradox but is not ; the same thing can be observed in every other department of culture. It is only surprising because people wrongly regard the English 'reading public' (and the art, musical and theatre-going public) as a unity, whereas that unity has ceased to exist since literature has become accessible to everybody. This observation applies to every nation, but the differences of level between the various sections of the public are much greater in England because classes are much more sharply distinguished there. Society, the middle classes and the lower classes live in different worlds, with a different education, different traditions and different tastes. As book-buyers the lower classes do not come into the picture, having no money to spare for that; another thing that keeps the editions of most books small is the admirably developed system of public lending-libraries; every nook and corner of England has one of these public libraries, but the complaints about the level of taste of their patrons are almost as numerous as they are themselves. The middle classes, which are beyond a doubt proportionately larger than in continental countries, constitute the largest reading public, and the character of the average literary product is dictated by them. Their taste is conventional: what they demand is well-bred puritanical commonplaces, sentimental nonsense or fatuous, half-concealed indecency, love stories with happy endings, tales of adventure and detective stories concocted according to recipes that have been tried out hundreds of times.

Literature worthy of the name is in England an affair of small circles. The people interested in it are :—a section of Society, university circles (especially at Oxford and Cambridge) and a section of the middle classes which is not easily defined and has nothing exactly corresponding to it on the Continent but has come just in the last few decades to set the tone. In Germany before the War the upper *bourgeoisie*, which formed the rich society of the Thiergarten quarter in Berlin, the industrial towns of the Rhineland and certain other big cities, was the real cultured class; materially at any rate they were the mainstay of art, literature and the theatre and pillars of culture, whether from motives of snobbery or conviction does not matter—a function which the corresponding classes in England do not feel any sort of obligation to fulfil. There it was much more the aristocracy, which is socially on a still higher level, that set the tone, and still sets it to-day, but it forms the conservative wing of the literary public; these people buy the weighty, solid memoirs and biographies of which there are so many in England, just as they buy old pictures and old china. In their attitude towards modern *belles lettres* they are cautious and not particularly interested; on the other hand one must not overlook the fact that the most important patrons of modern art, literature, drama and music have in all periods been, and still are to-day, aristocrats—exceptional phenomena, but exceptions that always seem to recur.

The left wing of the intellectuals comes from the so-called 'suburban' section of the middle class. 'The suburbs' means in this connection the well-to-do suburbs like Hampstead, Richmond etc., which, together with one or two more central districts like Chelsea, are inhabitated by a well-to-do, though according to English standards by no means rich, *bourgeoisie*—the really rich people do not live in the suburbs, which are not considered quite first-class socially. Writers, artists and academic people live in them, but the majority of their population consists of doctors, lawyers and business men. This 'suburban' society is the only society in England that feels itself under an obligation to be 'cultured,' thus resembling German *bourgeois* circles, whose qualities and defects it shares; it takes its aspirations very seriously and makes real sacrifices for them, but it is absolutely without any direct instinctive feeling for artistic values. It is intellectual and well-informed and knows what one must admire at the moment if one wants to be on the crest of the wave, and what one must condemn if one is not going to be old-fashioned, a thing which is almost equivalent to a loss of honour in these circles in both countries; in short, an element of snobbery forms an integral part of its enthusiasm. Now this class is highly unpopular, on account of the Englishman's exceptionally strong dislike of clap-trap and intellectual 'airs.' The word 'suburban' is accompanied by a slight wrinkling of the nostrils; it suggests something not quite genuine. People are reluctant to admit the really great importance of the suburbs for the intellectual life of the country; yet it is certain that without them modern literature and art would never have been able to make their way in England; for they alone have given them, in some ways, a reasonably broad footing. The suburbs secured the success of Shaw, Wells and Chesterton in England; they are to-day the best reading and theatre-going public and the promoters of modern pictorial art too.

They are, naturally, not the only ones; lovers of literature are to be found in all circles, but the 'suburbanites' are the only class that, collectively considered, shows a really strong interest in modern literature, which apart from them is an affair of small cliques and coteries. Every important writer or poet has his little circle of admirers and many of them find patrons too; patronage is very much alive in England, which is entirely in harmony with the English inclination to leave everything as far as possible to private enterprise. In Germany a man like Stefan George, whom his juniors accept as a poet of the first rank while the great public remains completely ignorant of him, is an exceptional phenomenon; but in England this kind of secret cult is nothing unusual, and many of the best authors write for small circles of that type. England has an extremely intelligent and exceedingly exacting literary public ; but it is small in numbers, while the great public is absolutely without intelligence or intellectual pretensions, England being even in intellectual matters an aristocratic country. Hence the great difficulty in the way of wide-spread success for any writer of importance. Shaw's position in England is typical of this : for many years he was unpopular with the great public because he was too revolutionary, unconventional and intellectual, and also with the minority, though for the opposite reasons, namely, that he was only too much the *bourgeois* puritanical preacher of moral sermons, a ridiculous tilter against windmills that had been knocked down long ago—till the Suburbs came to his rescue. The many really gifted writers of the present generation are little, if at all, known to the great public. As a rule, a new talent remains for a long time the private property of a small circle ; in most cases success with the general public does finally follow in the course of time ; but the case of Meredith is a proof that a writer may be placed in the very highest class by the critics and the select public, and yet live and die without being more than a name, with hardly any conception attaching to it, to the multitude.

XIII

THE THEATRE IN ENGLAND

The importance of the English theatre is for the most part under-rated abroad, and English drama enjoys a thoroughly bad reputation. People there certainly do recognize the great importance of certain individual dramatists—after all it is impossible to deny that Shakespear was an Englishman—but they account for them as exceptions, refusing to grasp the fact that in this nation of individualists exceptions are the rule. There is probably no European nation, with the possible exception of the Italians, that takes more pleasure in the theatre, in acting and in things dramatic. Modern drama, the drama of the individual, had its birth in England, and it was English strolling players who revived the dramatic art of Northern Europe. English drama took its start from the theatre, from the actors, not from literature like German classical drama; the English have had a sense of the drama from the very beginning.

It would, perhaps, be more correct to say that only a part of the nation has this sense. Here we see the schism introduced into the development of England by Puritanism. The Puritans considered the theatre almost as sinful as the Catholic Church, smelling paganism in both of them, not without grounds; it was not till the Restoration that the drama regained an honourable position, in which it continued to rank high until the Puritanism of the Victorian age brought it once more into disrepute. It was the middle classes that were particularly hostile to it in that period, considering it sinful, and vulgar into the bargain, to go to the theatre. Drama sank to its lowest level ; light operas and insipid comedies dominated the stage, while the tragedian Henry Irving and his partner Ellen Terry were almost the only people left who concerned themselves with Shakespear.

This period lasted long enough to allow the opinion to grow up that the English theatre was a negligible quantity. The great continental Naturalist movement passed by England without leaving a trace ; the greatest dramatist of the period, Ibsen, was only appreciated by a few, and as for English dramatists of importance, there were none, Pinero, the best known, being a feeble edition of Sardou. Irving's successor, Tree, was only a mediocre actor, but he was a great producer, and even Reinhardt at the beginning of his career was influenced by him. Even in the days of its deepest degradation the English theatre had its brighter side, in its splendid production and frequently excellent acting. Then comes the beginning of its transformation with Bernard Shaw, just about at the same time as the decay of Puritanism in the reign of Edward VII.

It is worth noting that since the War the English stage, in contrast to the state of things on the Continent, has beyond any doubt improved very much, an improvement in which the institution of the Stage Societies has played an important part. The Stage Societies are clubs which produce plays of literary merit in one or more performances, mostly on Sundays. As private concerns they are subject to no censorship, and it is not their business to make money, as all other theatrical productions have to in England, which, true to its individualism, has no national or subsidized theatre. The Stage Societies in their turn created a public which made literary demands on the theatre, and many dramatists got a hearing whose work the commercial theatres had turned down but frequently took over after it had been tried out. The result is that to-day a steady half-dozen theatres have something of merit from the literary point of view to offer. That may not seem a tremendous lot, but it implies very great progress as compared with pre-War times, and it implies, above all, a change of feeling.

The position of the London stage differs in many respects from that of the stage on the Continent. Not merely is there, as already stated, no subsidized theatre, but there are no longer any theatres owned by their managers. Before the War there was the system of the 'star' actor-manager; Tree, Wyndham, Alexander and the rest had their own theatres in which they naturally played the lead in every respect, just as Sarah Bernhardt, Réjane and others did in Paris. The day of the Stars seems to be over in both countries (while in Germany on the contrary a Star system unknown before the War has developed) and with them the actor-manager has disappeared too. The big London theatres belong to men of business who let them on lease, and the absurd pitch to which rents have increased is a great hindrance to the healthy development of the theatre, because it has meant an incredible increase in the risks. The producer —this field is dominated by one or two big figures— take a lease of a theatre for a fixed time, and a play which happens to succeed better than was expected often has to migrate to another one. Hence it comes about that the principal theatres have no sort of permanent features of their own; where Shakespear is played to-day one may see an American musical comedy to-morrow.

The principal playhouses, amounting to forty or fifty theatres and music-halls, are all crowded together in the West End; they are the only ones to which the visitor gets, and so he generally judges the English theatre by what they have to offer him, which chiefly consists of social or detective comedies with no aspirations to literary merit but for the most part very cleverly constructed : Noel Coward's and Frederick Lonsdale's plays, like *Hay-Fever* (describing a week-end) and *The Last of Mrs. Cheney*, which get produced in the very best theatres in Germany, are typical specimens. The acting is for the most part of a high order ; for, as a successful play of this sort may run continuously for a year or longer, it is worth while getting the best talent for every part. No less numerous than the plays of this type are the musical comedies, which to-day mostly come from America, as they did from Vienna before the War ; the setting is pretty and the performance slick, and the comedians, in whom England abounds, are invariably admirable. There will also be one or two thrillers, one or two farces, one or two pieces of old-fashioned sob-stuff and a number of revues ; probably also a Shakespear play and some play or other by Shaw or some young English playwright or even by some foreigner—that is, on an average, three or four interesting plays.

The performance is generally excellent, except in the case of Shakespear's tragedies, which are often acted in an entirely conventional way. England at present has a large number of actors who are excellent in comedy and in modern plays and innumerable comedians, but no tragedians of mark. Tragedy has remained outside the Englishman's beat ; the outbreaks of feeling which it involves run counter to his whole education, which is deliberately calculated to make him suppress his feelings, and when he tries his hand at it, he easily becomes declamatory or frigid. Figures like Richard III, Othello and Lady Macbeth cannot be reconciled with the ideals of the Lady and the Gentleman, and Shakespear and

Greek Tragedy (of which there are revivals from time to time) say nothing to the public of the West-End theatres, the only public we have so far considered, which is drawn from upper-class circles, innumerable visitors, and casual representatives of all ranks of society —is, in fact, the amusement public of all great cities, which goes to the theatre for the hour or two from dinner to supper and dancing and wants to be amused. In London it has at least the superior merit of looking nice and wearing evening dress, as the theatres have of possessing comfortable seats, good ventilation etc. These theatres put one in the way of a thoroughly agreeable light entertainment, which is all that is expected of them : for the rest, they are mostly very well attended and the seats are frequently all sold out ; an unsuccessful play disappears after a few performances. London apparently still has too few theatres of this type, and quite a number are at present under construction or projected.

Apart from the West-End theatres, however, London also possesses about an equal number of suburban and People's theatres which mostly remain quite unknown to strangers, while Londoners themselves in most cases only know the one in the district where they live ; for London is made up of many separate towns. It is characteristic that it should be practically impossible to get hold of a complete theatre list : the papers give only the West-End theatres and here and there a suburban one, poster-kiosks are unknown, and placards and advertisements are arbitrarily distributed. Here too the rule holds good that the fairest rose blushes unseen and only known to a few, while the generally known and popular things attain to no very high level ; for it is precisely in the suburbs and their theatres that the most interesting things in the theatrical world of London happen.

To begin with, however, one must get clear about the terms 'Suburban Theatre' and 'People's Theatre,' which by no means correspond to what people on the Continent understand by them. A 'suburban theatre' is not a suburban theatre in the continental sense because 'the suburbs' are not continental suburbs; they are much more villa colonies, but in saying that one must note that these settlements of self-contained houses are not inhabited by particularly rich people, like the Grunewald colony in Berlin, but by *bourgeois* ranging in countless gradations from middle fortune to great prosperity. High or rich Society does not live in the suburbs but in the smart parts of the West End or in the country. Now there are two different types of suburban theatre: the majority belong to large theatrical organizations and are pretty well standardized, the same play, musical comedy or even variety-show wandering from theatre to theatre. With few exceptions no place except London has permanent companies; they are all touring companies: if a play has a success in the Capital, often more than one company goes out into the provinces and even as far as the most distant colonies with it. Apart from them one also finds companies touring under the lead of a Star, and a certain number of self-contained companies are permanently on tour and in their turn visit London. The suburban theatres which belong to the big organizations are therefore provincial theatres visited by London companies. Your Croydon or New Cross man would rather see the West-End successes not quite so well produced in the local theatre from a cheap seat, or wait a year to see the Stars in their most brilliant parts, than undertake the long journey to and from theatre-land and pay the big prices that are the rule up there. This development in the theatrical world is the result of London's immense area, which makes it possible for a London company to spend many months touring Greater London.

Such is the first group of the suburban theatres, in which only the inhabitants of the suburbs concerned are interested. The second group, which has only sprung into existence in the last few years, is much less numerous but extremely interesting: it is here that the plays of the greatest literary value are to be seen to-day, which is due partly to the character of the population of certain suburbs and partly to the relatively small cost of running that sort of theatre. These theatres have a character of their own and, since they also have their regular public, they can risk experiments. Hampstead possesses one of this kind where plays by young English writers are included in the repertoire side by side with Shaw, Chesterton etc. There is a theatre at Kew that specialises in Russian plays under the influence of the famous Moscow producer, Komissarjevsky, and one at Hammersmith where admirable performances of Restoration and eighteenth-century comedies are to be seen. These theatres often produce plays which are subsequently taken up by the West-End theatres, and it is to them and the Stage Societies that the credit for the improvement in public taste which has set in since the War is due.

The real People's theatres are to be found, in ever-decreasing numbers, in the working-class districts. With one solitary exception they do not care tuppence about literary quality, but they are the most genuine and primitive element left in the theatrical life of England and probably of the whole of Europe. Here, before a working-class audience that smokes and feels thoroughly at home, permanent companies composed of people personally well-known to the audience perform melodramas often written by one of themselves. They are good strong thrillers, full of murder and sudden death, persecuted innocence, rescuing heroes, villains and intrigues, but invariably also full of the most genuinely humorous comic scenes of popular life. The audience is exceedingly enthusiastic, joins in eagerly and absolutely loses itself in what is going on ; prudery is unknown and strong emotion of any kind is welcomed. One gets the impression that the audience has hardly changed since Shakespear's time and that the only thing that is wanting is the great poet, and the rightness of this impression is proved by the existence and success of the Old Vic., the ancient playhouse situated in a poor quarter on the south side of the river, which performed melodramas like the rest of its kind, till it occurred to a few enthusiasts for the drama to put the real thing before this public instead of the feeble caricature of an imitation. The success was astonishing and the public took its cue enthusiastically ; to this part of the population of London Shakespear is as thrilling and interesting as he was in the days when he trod the boards himself, just close by the Old Vic. Here beyond all doubt is the only genuine Shakespearean stage and Shakespearean public in existence, far from all literary experiments, triumphs of the producer's art and star actors ; here one feels that the drama might once more become a concern of the English people. In addition to Shakespear Mozart's operas, as well as a number of old English plays, have been produced at the Old Vic. with no less success—indeed, the material success has been so great that there is a movement to found a similar theatre in the North of London.

Even so this does not exhaust all the various aspects of the London stage. To return, first of all, to some of the companies, briefly touched on already, that tour London as well as the provinces, which means that they are often to be seen in the Capital for many months of the year : some are of a purely provincial character like Benson's Shakespear company, which, though meritorious, is not up to London standards, and the Carl Rosa company, which does opera in English. These mostly keep to the suburbs ; on the other hand the operatic company which does nothing but the works of Gilbert and Sullivan is extremely popular in the West End too. The light operas of Gilbert and Sullivan, which date from the 'eighties, have become a permanent institution, as Offenbach's, for instance, might be in France ; their satirical librettos are still amusing to-day and their music has retained its charm. These English touring companies with a strictly defined repertoire are an historic relic of the early days of the modern stage and they have their great advantages : if the theatrical system established in the provinces has the advantage of being able to offer a large repertoire, this sort of touring company has a first-rate team of specialists. In England anyhow they are now, as in the past, a very important element in the theatrical life of the country, and new companies of the kind are constantly springing up. Thus a very good company that only plays Shaw has been in existence for a number of years ; also a quite first-rate Irish company, the *Irish Players*, which acts plays by young Irish writers and has conspicuously helped to secure a big success in London for the playwright O'Casey : it is an offshoot of the famous theatre in Dublin which confines itself to the first production of Irish plays and is based on the co-operation of writers, actors and stage-decorators—a new sort of community-theatre. There is another company which carries its own motor stage about with it and performs primarily in little places which have no theatre. The importance of all these companies is due to the fact that so few towns have a theatre with a permanent company. Among these exceptions are Liverpool and Birmingham and recently Cambridge, which can boast a first-rate modern literary theatre ; in Cambridge as in Oxford, there are, besides, several productions every year by undergraduate actors, sometimes of Greek tragedies in the original, which are often surprisingly good. Finally we must not forget the immense number of amateur companies scattered all over the country. The Englishman's growing keenness on the theatre here shows itself clearly and in a manner very characteristic of the nation, i.e. actively. It is particularly the newly erected garden-cities that have taken the lead in this movement ; they invariably possess one or more amateur companies which mostly cultivate modern drama.

Thus the impression that the West-End stage gives of the state of the theatre in England is a false, or at least a partial, one. It is true of this sphere, as of every other, that in England the most valuable things are hidden away and have to be looked for and that they calmly and obstinately go their own way, which is not that of the multitude. The West-End theatres which everyone knows are commercial enterprises ; plays of any value are seldom to be seen in them, and their standard, except for their good acting, is lower than in other countries where the theatre counts. As against that, the Stage Societies, People's theatres, certain suburban theatres, certain touring companies and amateur companies, all in their various kinds reveal a strong, genuine, idealistic and disinterested passion for the theatre such as can be seen in no other European country with the possible exception of Russia.

The London music-halls also differ in many ways from similar places on the Continent. Interest in revue has fallen off sharply, and only actors of exceptional drawing-power can make a success of it ; and the West-End music-halls have suffered an equally sharp decline of popularity—so much so that the most famous of them, the Empire, has actually been pulled down. They get crowded out by the gigantic theatres of the Coliseum or Palladium type, whose programmes are notably more various but have less character. Everything can be had there, for they cater for the widest masses ; the Coliseum, for instance, holds five thousand people and has two performances daily : one gets sketches with famous actors in them, Ballet (the Russian Ballet often appeared there), full orchestras, even operas ; but only an occasional real music-hall artist appears in the programme. These theatres have anyhow solved the problem of providing an entertainment which interests all classes at an incredibly low price and of producing perpetual novelties—as a rule the programme changes every week. There are still a few music-halls (in the old sense) in the West End and a large number in the suburbs, most of them belonging to one or two big concerns which also dominate the Provinces. Here one still finds a great variety of talents : everything to do with acrobats is of course international ; on the other hand the innumerable low comedians of both sexes are genuinely English and represent the ancient English tradition of the clown. This kind of talent never seems to die out, and its most brilliant representative, Charlie Chaplin, who began as a music-hall low comedian, has carried it over into the Films.

The cinema is the most dangerous enemy especially of the small, lower-class music-halls, which have gone down before it in large numbers. Its friends and enemies alike must admit the fact that it has a levelling effect : its productions in London are exactly the same as its productions in Paris, New York or Peking, and the standard of taste of the great public is also obviously on the same low level everywhere. London has lately acquired a Film Society which strives, in the manner of the Stage Societies, to set before its members only films of artistic interest at which the cinemas will not look, with the object of thus educating public taste. But the difficulties are very great ; there is certainly no lack of interest, but there is a lack of films of real merit. English film production is, as is well known, insignificant, and it is only recently that any attempt has been made to raise its level.

Cabaret, in the continental sense, has never got a firm footing in England ; but now, when it seems to be dying out even in Paris, it is beginning to flourish to a certain extent in London. A number of big hotels and restaurants have developed a form of after-theatre evening entertainment which consists of supper, dancing and cabaret turns. It is primarily a matter of exhibition dancing, but one may also come across very competent *raconteurs*, *diseuses* and burlesquers on these occasions. The same sort of thing, on a smaller scale but of the very best quality, is to be seen in one or two small and very smart supper places. These hybrids are also highly characteristic of England : the Englishman instinctively demands a chance to be active ; he wants to take part in the show himself—in other words, he has a primitive passion for the theatre which only the Italian shares with him. The audience at a music-hall likes joining in the songs, which is the original foundation of the whole thing, just as it joins in the play at the People's theatres, and in these suppers with cabaret, the turns alternate with the audience's own activities in dancing and amusing itself.

The theatre used to be a popular art in England ; its connection with the Court in the Restoration period was quite transitory, and even then it was very popular in tone. The nineteenth, the *bourgeois*, century discovered the theatre as an educational institution and a forum for the discussion of social or moral questions, especially in Germany, Scandinavia and Russia, and it became intellectual. This epoch coincides with the eclipse of the theatre in England, because only very small circles in the upper middle class supported that sort of drama; it was too bloodless (in every sense) for popular consumption and too heavy and serious for Society; people preferred their 'problems,' like their literature, in book form. It is characteristic that the most important playwright of this movement, Bernard Shaw, provides his plays with long prefaces which are often the most interesting thing in them. What real dramatist—Shakespear or Aeschylus, Molière or Calderon—can one conceive writing philosophical explanatory prefaces? Middle-class rationalism and dramatic instinct cannot live together, and the middle-class age found its literary account in the novel.

It would be odd if the present more impulsive revolutionary period did not bring the theatre new strength once more; up to date there is a strong opposition between the intellectual and literary drama, which is still accepted as the highest form of art, and these strivings towards a renewal of the theatre which are cropping up everywhere. These have as yet developed no form, but their efforts are in the direction of rhythmical movement of the body, mastery of space, and a dynamic and musical condition; they are entirely anti-literary, but thoroughly of the theatre and thoroughly dramatic. This 'Liberated Theatre,' as Tairof has called it, is very closely related to English popular melodrama, English low comedy and English acrobatic dancing (e.g. the chorus girls), and it is by no means unlikely that it will find its form in England.

XIV

THE PRESS

EVERY country has the press it deserves, only its press seldom exhibits such unity of character that one can safely draw conclusions from it concerning the general features of the nation. The English press presents an appearance as rich in contradictions and rival interpretations as the English character. It is in many respects the best, and in several respects the worst, in Europe, and while its highest achievements are unsurpassed, in its lowest parts it almost gets down to the American pattern.

The *Times* is as much the pattern and model of the great political opinion-forming newspapers of all countries as the Parliament of Westminster is the pattern and the mother of all parliaments. The *Times*, and some other big English newspapers too are exemplary in almost every respect; there are only two things in which the best Paris papers are superior to them, clear arrangement of matter and the *feuilleton*. The *Times* is a Great Power, its correspondents are ambassadors and its world-wide standing is unique; it belongs, together with the Bank of England, the Navy and Parliament, to the immovable foundations of England's existence. It could afford to be more expensive than any other paper and need make no concessions to the bad taste of the masses; all it needs to do is to remain true to its traditions. It has its own political policy, mostly in agreement with the Foreign Office but sometimes in opposition to its plans. It is essentially Conservative, but its policy is not laid down along the lines of any party. Its leading articles are unsigned ; no journalist, however eminent, may speak in his own person here ; authority is of the *Times* as such.

Its political and war correspondents have often had a decisive influence in European politics ; they are all over the place, and the news-service of the *Times* is unsurpassed ; anyone who reads it carefully is informed on everything that is going on in the sphere of politics and economics all over the world. To read it like that takes a long time, and it is a paper that makes great demands of its readers, a paper that addresses itself to a select few. Its circulation is probably negligible compared with those of the sensational papers ; for it is intended for the ruling class, not the masses. It is read by politicians, ministers, the leading figures in commerce and industry, by magistrates and officials, and the potentates who occupy the great country houses, the offices from which great enterprises are controlled and the leading positions all over the British Empire ; and that is enough. In spheres of secondary importance it can also afford to give its readers nothing but the best ; it is in a position to finance big expeditions, get articles from the really important people all over the world, and produce, in its *Literary Supplement*, the most important literary periodical in the country. It stands above competition, and the journalists of every country speak of it with reverential awe, in the way Catholics speak of Rome and smart women of the *Haute Couture* of Paris. The *Times* is majestic, weighty, impressive, massive as a dreadnought, not a newspaper as other newspapers are, but a national institution, exceedingly characteristic of the traditional aristocratic England of the ruling classes, of the minority which in spite of its small numbers still rules the roost to-day.

The *Morning Post* and the *Daily Telegraph* are externally hardly less impressive than the *Times*, with the same gigantic page, great bulk and good print. They too are papers of the minority, the ultra-Conservative *Morning Post* being Society's paper, while the City rather leans towards the *Telegraph*. They are both high-class, well-edited papers, but not unique phenomena like the *Times*; they play the Cardinals to the Pope of the *Times*. Into the same category comes the *Manchester Guardian*, the only provincial paper that can compete with the London papers: in tradition and importance it is not unlike the *Frankfurter Zeitung*, being like it the leading paper of a wealthy commercial city and like it liberal and democratic. Among the evening papers the *Evening Standard*, though not up to the standard of the great morning papers, is the best.

This group of newspapers represents the old England; they date back to the days when reading the newspapers, in common with all reading, was the privilege of the upper classes, and it is to these classes that they address themselves. Their aspect is Victorian, solid, reliable and well-to-do; the 'leisured classes' is an English term for designating these classes of Society, and indeed the study of these papers demands leisure and peace of mind. They are discreet, calm and respectable, like the mahogany furniture and the solid houses in the classical style of the first half of the nineteenth century, and they constitute a proof that this traditional England has by no means bowed itself out yet. The arrangement of their contents gives away a lot about the English character. First of all come politics, with an excellent news-service from every quarter of the globe, weighty leading articles and many contributions by prominent people—the last a truly British institution. Next to politics come finance and commerce, then sport;

literature, the drama, music and art take the place which England assigns to them, i.e. by no means the first, as in many Paris papers, but an important one. The *feuilleton* in the continental sense ('below the line') is unknown. There is a lot of social news, detailed law reports, excellent weather forecasts and first-rate articles by specialists in every sphere. The outside sheets are covered with innumerable advertisements; the middle pages are the most important ones, and the arrangement of the rest of the contents is frequently very far from clear; after all there is plenty of time.

The man who revolutionized English journalism was Alfred Harmsworth, later known as Lord Northcliffe. He grasped the fact that an extensive class of uneducated readers had come into existence and gave it what it demanded—cheap sensation. His paper was cheap: when he started the *Daily Mail*, the *Times* was fourpence, the other papers a penny. The *Mail* was a halfpenny; It had to have an immense circulation if it was to pay, and it got it. The *Mail* and the papers like it stand out in the sharpest contrast to the old-established English newspapers, being superficial, unreliable, strident, vulgar and sensational. The *Mail* is as much below the level of the continental newspaper as the *Times* is above it, and the state of affairs by which Harmsworth for a time owned them both was one that is only conceivable in journalism

The *Mail* became the model not only for English papers but for many continental ones too, and its influence is as great as it is baleful. It is, in its way, brilliantly put together, for it understands the art of pandering to the instincts of the great masses; it requires no effort of the brain to read it, all the articles being short and wholly superficial, but amusing, snappily written and with a punch in them. Everything in it is sensational and coloured by a certain point of view : it is jingoistic and must always have some foreign enemy against whom it uses any and every means of attack, professedly in the interests of the country and its poor, innocent, unsuspicious readers. It must have a hate on : for many years the red rag was Germany, now it is the Bolsheviks. There is no exaggeration too crude, no argument too feeble, to be used in this war ; the fact that this press campaign is not much more effective than it is is astonishing and bears witness to the sound common sense of the English. Of course there are enemies at home who get it in the neck too, like the Socialists who mean to divide up everybody's fortune, the Chancellors of the Exchequer who mean to increase taxation, the War Ministers who never show enough energy in looking after the strength of the Army and the Navy—in short, everything that is already unpopular on its own account.

The gaps are filled up with news of the latest sensations, i.e. athletic records, murders and business scandals ; but they are also exceedingly loyal and full of information about the life of the most highly placed personages. The reader is intended to get the feeling of being on intimate terms with earls, dukes and Princes of the Blood ; he knows all about their private lives, and you may be sure they correspond to his idea of them, according to which all these grand people know no higher ambition than to live and think exactly like Mr. and Mrs. Smith and the children in their suburban villa. How well and happy the Prince of Wales feels among the gallant workers of the East End (picture inset) ! What a touchingly good mother the lovely Duchess is ! How nice and simple and homely the great statesman is sitting by the fire with his pipe ! It is a truly rosy world and just what the unscrupulous villain of an enemy is out to upset. There is also a lot of correspondence on everyday problems—What is the right age for marriage? Is the Modern Girl less virtuous than previous generations ? (Of course not; she has a heart of gold.)—a lot of sporting news, some fashions and cookery, a little talk about art and the theatre so far as there is anything in any way sensational about them, amusing short sketches and, above all, lots of pictures.

Pictures are the most powerful enemy of the paper with standards, and nothing gives away the level of the reading public so thoroughly as the way in which pictures in newspapers and magazines have caught on, a phenomenon that has, incidentally, made its appearance in Germany during the last few years in an even more catastrophic fashion than in Anglo-Saxon countries. What is happening to us is a regression to the picture-writing of primitive peoples ; the picture, which can be immediately grasped, is crowding out the word, which requires mental effort to understand it, and the more important a place the illustrations take, the more the habit of reading, and with it of thinking, gets lost. The daily paper consisting almost exclusively of pictures is also a creation of the father of the *Daily Mail* : the *Daily Mirror* and its rival the *Daily Sketch* have cut their printed matter down to the absolute minimum ; they convey information by means of pictures and bad ones at that, as is inevitable in mass-production.

Of late years the mantle of Lord Northcliffe has descended to some extent upon the shoulders of Lord Beaverbrook, the owner of the *Daily Express*, rather than upon those of Lord Rothermere, the present owner of the *Daily Mail*. It is sensational as the *Daily Mail* and its politics are even more cleverly served up in a welter of sentimentality and clap-trap which makes no demands upon the brain of the average reader. The circulation of the *Daily Mail* remains the larger of the two, but the *Daily Express* is probably the greater political force.

The position of the more serious papers which are out for a large circulation and hence must not be more expensive than the Northcliffe papers, is a difficult one. The *Daily Chronicle*,[1] the *Daily News* and the *Daily Herald*[2] are, on the whole, reliable, decent and well-informed, but they are compelled to imitate the scare headlines, illustrations and fatuities of the *Mail* in order to be able to compete with it. It is easy to see why none of them achieves the huge popular success of the *Mail*; the fact is that they are cross-breeds. The *Daily News* is the paper of the non-conformist middle classes and is financed by wealthy Quakers; the *Chronicle* was once Lloyd George's organ and subsequently Lord Reading's, and the *Herald* is the only Labour paper; probably none of the three could survive without their backers and subsidies from party funds. It is, incidentally, highly characteristic of England that its immense working class has only one solitary party organ, and that it has none too many readers either [2] beyond a doubt, the great masses read the reactionary jingo Northcliffe papers, but election results prove that they do not allow themselves to be in any way influenced by the politics of those papers. Here we have a truly English paradox and a proof that it is easy to over-rate the real influence of the press; the masses obviously only read what amuses them, i.e. sporting news and law-court and Society gossip and so on; as regards politics, they remain uninfluenced. Of the three evening papers the *Evening News*, a Northcliffe paper, has far the widest circulation; the *Evening Standard* must be numbered among the educated papers,

[1] Written before the recent 'merger' with the *Daily News*.
[2] Recently reorganized and made more moderate in political tone. Its circulation has sinced increased.

the Liberal evening paper, the *Star*, belongs to the same category as the *Evening News*, and there is no Labour evening paper at all. It is safe to say that about half of England reads Northcliffe in the evening, but most of it only the racing and football results.

The Sunday papers are a chapter to themselves. Special papers of prodigious bulk appear in England on Sundays, not on Mondays as in Germany. Among these the cleavage between the educated and the popular papers is still deeper. The *Observer* and the *Sunday Times* are great and admirably conducted papers; Garvin, the editor of the *Observer*, counts as the most important political journalist in England, and his articles are exceedingly influential, while the reviews in these papers, their articles on drama, art and literature, are also a decisive force. The *Referee* is the most important theatrical paper in the country. The numerous other Sunday papers, such as the *Empire News*, the *News of the World* and *Reynolds's*, vie with one another in sensation-mongering and bad taste, with their columns of stuff about murders and accidents, their frankly shrieking headlines and the excessive platitudinousness and fatuity of their matter. They constitute the strangest, and by no means fortuitous, obbligato to the organ tones of Puritan sabbatarianism.

Anyone who is doubtful about the great contrast between the upper class and the great masses in England, a contrast which certainly is never stressed but hushed up as much as possible, has only to study the press, in which he will find the social structure clearly mirrored and from which he will gather the advantages and disadvantages of a system which aims not at equality but at the highest possible cultivation of those destined for it, and will see that the mental pabulum of the few is as different from that of the many as their education, the way they live and the spheres of activity open to them are.

What I have said about the daily papers applies to the periodicals too : England has the best, and the worst, periodicals in Europe ; but this needs to be qualified by the observation that no other country has so many high-class periodicals, so many tolerable and relatively so few inferior ones, which means that periodicals are read a lot by the upper classes and not much by the masses. The admirable weeklies are a feature peculiar to England. The *Saturday Review*, the *Spectator*, the *Nation*, the *New Statesman*, the *Week End Review* and the rest of them, are political papers of great significance, in which men like Shaw and Keynes —to mention only world-famous names——say their say ; their importance is, however, by no means confined to the sphere of politics but extends, both in their critical articles and in their original contributions, to art, literature and science. They are roughly and approximately the equivalent of German papers like the *Tagebuch* and the *Weltbühne* ; only they have incomparably greater resources at their disposal and are more closely connected with the political parties. If one reads one of these weeklies one can give up reading the daily papers without missing anything essential. England is also very well provided with good monthlies ; the *English Review*, the *Contemporary* and the *Nineteenth Century*, and the *Quarterly*, the *Edinburgh Review*[1] and the *Hibbert Journal*— the last three being quarterlies—are all weighty publications which treat of political, cultural, scientific and artistic questions, besides bringing out original literary contributions ; and they too are unsurpassed anywhere in quality and quantity. In the way of purely literary monthlies there are the *London Mercury*, the *New*

---

[1] Ceased publication a few months ago.

Adelphi and the quarterly *Criterion*; they are quite as excellent, if not quite so numerous, as the French ones, while Germany has little to compare with them except the *Neue Rundschau*. The *Burlington Magazine*, the *Connoisseur* and the *Studio* are world-famous art papers, but in this department there is room for a good paper devoted to modern art. There are of course also innumerable specialist papers, and the serious character of English periodical journalism deserves the highest admiration.

Descending a step in the intellectual scale we find a very large number of illustrated weeklies which are excellent in their way. The classic examples of this breed are the *Graphic*, the *Sphere* and the *Illustrated London News*, high-class Conservative papers whose stuff, whether in the form of printed matter or pictures, is worthy to rank with that of the great dailies—Chesterton has been a contributor to the *Illustrated London News* for years; with illustrations from all over the world at their command, they are typical papers of an imperial nation. The *Bystander*, the *Tatler*, the *Sketch*, and the *Sporting and Dramatic* are less serious-minded and more superficial and amusing, Society, the stage and sport being their staple subjects. It is an easy transition from them to the papers like *Vogue*, the *Queen* etc., which are primarily fashion papers, more or less in the manner of *Die Dame* in Berlin. The magazines—an English invention—are not particularly numerous and hardly better than the continental imitations. The best known of them is the *Strand Magazine*, which brought out Kipling, Jerome and Conan Doyle and raised the short story to the level of a work of art; most of the rest attach the greatest importance to pictures of more or less attractive girls, and their articles and stories are calculated to please a thoroughly simple-minded public.

England possesses only one comic paper worth mentioning, *Punch*, and even *Punch* is not a comic paper in the continental sense. *Punch* is the *Times* of humour ; like the *Times*, it is intended for a quite definite social class and is, like it, a national institution. The *Punch* political cartoon is appreciated not for its artistic but for its political significance and may exercise a great influence, and the comments on political, social and artistic matters are to be taken seriously. *Punch* has its traditions and its standards, both very charactersitically English : it always keeps within the limits prescribed by social life and never outrages accepted good taste ; it never indulges in *double entendre*, coarseness or even discourtesy and is invariably fit for society. Hence it is severely limited, but within those limits, no paper in the world comes up to it in subtlety and literary standard. Its jokes are often not up to much and its drawings are mostly commonplace—there are exceptions like Phil May's in the past and Belcher's to-day—but its subtle irony is unsurpassable. *Punch* stands entirely alone ; the other so-called comic papers are on the lowest level of fatuity, cheap publications for a public which is exceedingly easy to please.

It was to this easily-satisfied public that *Answers*, the first paper Northcliffe started and the foundation-stone of his power and fortune, was dedicated. I do not believe that any other country of Europe has ever produced such a childish paper. It is cheap, badly printed, indescribably fatuous and extremely popular. Its 'answers' are on the level of the advice column in the lowest provincial papers : May a young girl allow her boy to kiss her, and if so where ? How can I get rid of freckles ? Shall I go on the stage or learn typing ? and so on. Next door to these there are bits of statistical information, e.g. if all the beer bottles emptied during a year in England were set one on top of the other they would reach exactly two and a half times as high as Mount Everest; short stories in which they marry and live happily ever after —always quite innocently, of course; and moving stories from the life of the Royal Family and the aristocracy. It is a paper for shop-girls and their young men and offers them a picture of the world which for fictitiousness, insipidity and sentimentality is only equalled by the cinema. *Answers* has of course found plenty of imitators and competitors, some of which tend rather in the direction of the comic paper, like the *London Opinion*, for instance, or the *London Mail*, which are smart in a cheap way, like artificial silk stockings; while others are rather calculated to appeal to lower-middle-class domesticity, like *Home Chat*, with its patterns for crochet work and advice to mothers on whether a baby shall wear a pink bow or a blue. A new note was struck by Horatio Bottomley in his paper *John Bull*, in which he posed as the Saviour of his country and the enemy of corruption and slackness, though it was new only in these cheap weeklies; he made a very great success of it, until he came to grief.

Thus a survey of English periodicals confirms what the survey of newspapers, literature and the theatre have demonstrated—that is, the immense differences in level between the different social classes in England, and thereby the fundamentally aristocratic character of the country. One cannot return too often to the point that it is impossible to make any general pronouncement about England and the English; one must always add which section of society one is discussing and to what class one is alluding; there can never be any question anywhere of a general level or a generally correct characterization. That applies in a lesser degree to other nations too, but anyone who is looking for the antithesis of England should consider Soviet Russia and he will then discover that it is not political differences but diametrically opposed ideals and attitudes to life that are the decisive factors in the opposition between Russia and England.

XV

ENGLAND AND EUROPE

ENGLAND has gone her own way and displays her individual character in every sphere : in government as in education, in her press as in her social structure, one always comes upon the same essential fundamental features, and all manifestations of the English spirit are instantly recognizable as such and different from those of other European nations. What is the relation between them ? Which predominates, kinship or contrast ? What is England's position in regard to Europe, and what do they mean to each other ? Is England a part of Europe or is it independent of the Continent or does it partly belong to it ? These are questions that are not easily answered, for England's relations to Europe are open to as many interpretations as everything else about it.

In a general way, England and the Continent regard each other in different ways. In the continental view England is one of the countries that make up the entity Europe ; in the Englishman's eyes all the European countries make up the entity which he calls ' the Continent ' and in which he does not count his own country. The Continent is not merely more foreign to him than any part of his great Empire, but more foreign even than the United States. In Melbourne or Montreal, Capetown or Bombay, he feels at home ; in New York or San Francisco he feels he is among relations ; but on the Continent, in Paris or Berlin or Warsaw or Madrid, he feels a stranger in a strange land, geographical proximity being overbalanced by cultural distance. The Continental looks upon England as a European country with 'colonies' in every quarter of the globe, whereas it is first and foremost the centre of the Anglo-Saxon world, though not only that—here too ambiguity, dual character and compromise prevail. England belongs to Europe without quite belonging to it ; it lives in a state of continuous reciprocal action with the Continent, but is not a part of it. It was once a part of Europe, but as it developed it moved away from Europe and is moving farther every day.

Mediaeval Gothic England was a European country, part of a whole, and it shared in the Renaissance ; subsequent movements and events in Europe did still find an echo in it, but they were directed into other channels there and issued in different *dénouements*. The Reformation, which rent Europe asunder so that the gash is not yet healed to-day, ended in a compromise in England. The Church of England is Protestant inasmuch as it does not recognize the authority of the Pope, but it is also Catholic inasmuch as it has preserved almost all the Catholic forms and looks upon itself as carrying on the Catholic tradition; it is, in fact, a national Catholic Church, a formula of compromise which put an end to the continuation of bitter doctrinal disputes. This was the first exclusively English solution of a European problem and, though it had no influence on other European countries, it was decisive for England. By the time of the Thirty Years' War, from which Germany has never quite recovered, England is already an almost completely neutral outsider, and from this time onwards the dissensions of Europe no longer break in directly on her, nor do the solutions that she finds for her problems exercise a direct influence on the Continent.

The Puritan movement is the English parallel to the wars of Religion on the Continent, but what a difference in methods, aims and results ! England here achieved in a few months the development which cost the Continent centuries ; after the victory of Cromwell England was living in a different epoch from the continental nations. The English people put an end to the Divine Right of Kings by executing their sovereign, secured the predominance of the elected parliament over the government and the army for all time to come and invested it with supremacy in financial matters. Set-backs did occur, but the great principles were established beyond the possibility of disturbance. Thus the English Revolution anticipated everything that the French Revolution was to produce later ; but it is just here that one sees England's exceptional position : the Continent remained absolutely unaffected by these events in England, and a hundred years later tuppeny-ha'penny German princelings could still sell their subjects and the King of France was responsible only to God, while the parliamentary system was unknown, the army a tool belonging to the sovereign and financial matters dependent on his personal caprice. On the outbreak of the French Revolution all the thrones of Europe trembled, but they all steadied themselves again the moment the son of the Revolution, Napoleon, was annihilated.

The French Revolution is certainly unthinkable without the example of England, but centuries passed before Voltaire and Montesquieu brought over from England the intellectual weapons for the struggle against the Church and the monarchy in France. England was beyond a doubt the political schoolmaster of Europe, but had she quite belonged to Europe her example would have had an immediate effect : her influence on Europe may be compared with the American influence that is so strong to-day. England for her part has remained, like America, untouched by events on the Continent. She took little interest in the great French Revolution and did not understand it ; far from seeing anything akin to her own history in it, she disapproved of the upheaval in other countries because the antecedents for such an upheaval were lacking in England itself. It was Napoleon's threat to her command of the sea and the danger of his uniting the Continent against her that first set England actively interfering in the destinies of Europe, and when the curtain had fallen on the tragedy of Napoleon, England also withdrew her hand from European affairs. She remained undisturbed by the reaction in Europe, and the revolutions of 1830 and 1848, though their object was to put English doctrines into practice, passed by without involving her at all. She was so detached that she could afford to be tolerant, and provided a refuge for everyone—for the exiled Orléans King, as later for the exiled Bonaparte, but equally for the revolutionaries and victims of political persecutions from every country.

Nineteenth-century England looked upon the political and social changes and upheavals of the Continent as none of her business, having other things to think about ; she was developing into the first industrial and commercial power in the world and collecting material for the British Empire : she was, in fact, once more living in a different epoch. Politically speaking she regarded Europe as an external entity from which she selected rulers or nations as allies or enemies according to her interests at the moment ; economically she was conquering the globe and thereby also becoming dependent on every quarter of it. Europe is an important, perhaps the most important, market for England but by no means her only one. She has developed on her own lines; while every other country clung to Protection, because they all saw their ideal in the self-supporting state, which has long been obsolete and impracticable, England adopted Free Trade. She imported from the whole world and exported to the whole world, quietly letting her agriculture decay if other countries could produce more cheaply, took the final steps in the transition to the modern industrial state and got a start of fifty years. Subsequently, when her success led to universal imitation and the whole world followed her example, she began to feel it: the days of England's absolute commercial supremacy were over; America and Germany caught up and in many respects left their model behind. Universal industrialization and economic rivalry led to the World War, in which England once more played a part in the destinies of Europe, but the dissensions which led to it and the consequences which followed it extend far beyond Europe. Even the World War was not primarily a European question for England: she entered it in order to combat the threatening competition of the German fleet and, as a secondary consideration, of German commerce and industry; but the fruits of her victory can be seen in Mesopotamia, Palestine and Africa. In the few years since the War she has already re-established tolerable relations with Germany, taken up her traditional attitude of neutrality to Franco-German quarrels and succeeded in regaining her position as arbiter; on the other hand she has returned to her equally traditional anti-Russian policy, which is now called 'the struggle with Bolshevism.' She is going her own way and Europe has once more become a side-issue for her; it is true that the political and economic destinies of all countries are interdependent, but that of England is more closely bound up with those of Asia,

Africa, America and Australia and more dependent on them than on those of Europe.

Culturally England has undoubtedly been a part of Europe right down to the present day; for centuries she was the recipient of continental culture, and from the Normans to the Renaissance and down to William of Orange, civilization in England derived its sustenance from the great continental streams. But from the time when she began to seek her destiny outside Europe the continental influence began to decline, while she on her side began influencing Europe—Shakespear is the father of modern drama, as the English eighteenth-century novelists are of the European novel—and her political institutions, the parliamentary system and the freedom of the press, conquered Europe. After the French Revolution England became the guiding spirit of Europe and during the nineteenth century blazed new trails down which other countries followed her; the age of coal and industrialization began, and railways and steamships created new conditions of life. England paid no attention to Europe but Europe gazed intently at England where these modern ideas came from, and every European country to a greater or less degree took over from England its commercial and industrial system, parliamentary government and Liberalism, its type of newspaper and its organization of trade. The one-sided conception of England as a merely commercial country, which is still universal on the Continent, dates from this period; by the side of its obvious strides in material progress its intellectual achievements got overlooked.

English literature, and still more English art, may have remained without influence on the Continent in this period—even to-day several of the greatest Victorian writers like Browning, Meredith and Hardy, are as good as unknown there ; but, to make up for that, since the end of the nineteenth century the influence of English civilization on the Continent has been getting steadily stronger. England was no doubt most remote from Europe in the 'sixties and 'seventies: the Paris of the Second Empire influenced the whole of Europe but not Victorian England, and while the Continent was passing through a sort of coarser Rococo period (see the furniture and clothes of the period), England was in the throes of the most puritanical epoch since Cromwell. Nobody knew what English life was like, and people regarded it as a blend of hypocrisy, piety and commercialism. The change was very gradual at first but proportionately more thorough. The majority of Frenchmen and Germans have doubtless never been conscious how completely they have adopted the ideals of English civilization, having made them so completely their own that they have forgotten their origin. With the exception of horse-racing, which had been imported from England in the eighteenth century, the idea of Sport was quite unknown on the Continent ; to-day it is one of the most important aspects of life and is given a place of honour in every newspaper. The Englishman, having not yet been able to get used to the victory of his ideal, is surprised that anyone but an Englishman should be keen on athletics and excel at them. The point is not merely that the whole of Europe and white people all over the rest of the world go in for tennis, football, boxing, golf, polo etc. and that people take a passionate interest in them ; the point is that they have brought about a revolution in education, sexual life and general attitude. Thirty years ago the athletic Englishwoman, a hearty epicene creature in men's clothes, with none of the feminine curves people loved so much, was a recognized subject for the caricaturist ; to-day the whole feminine ideal has been unconsciously metamorphosed into her type. Any woman who has hips and a bust, instead of reminding one of a boy, and does not know how to wear sports clothes is hopelessly un-modern and provincial ; the type of the English Girl has carried all before it in real life as well as on the stage, and with her the English Boy—where are the moustaches, the high stiff collars, the officer-type of yesterday now ? The youthful athletic type which comes from England is the ideal to which even greybeards aspire. It is impossible to go into details here, but enough has been said to make it obvious that athletics have altered the whole conduct of life and that open-air life, the unconstrained intercourse of the sexes, which has caused a change in the position of women, the decay of intellectual interests and so on are very intimately connected with them. The younger generation in every country of Europe and in almost all circles to-day resembles the English one, and this has happened solely through the continental type's assimilating itself to the English—not, that is, by mutual interaction but through the influence of one side only.

All modern social forms, not merely athletics, come from England and have so completely ousted the continental ones, at least as far as the upper classes are concerned, that people on the Continent have long regarded them as indigenous. To-day social life is English, as in the eighteenth century it was French ; and in those days French ideas of life probably seemed as little foreign and as much a matter of course to the people of the period as English ones do to-day. The eighteenth century built its Versailles for its rulers ; we build hotels de luxe for ours to-day. The Ritz-Carltons of London, Paris, Biarritz, St. Moritz, Deauville, Vienna and Baden Baden are the castles of our rulers—and who to-day stops to reflect that the modern hotel was invented in England, that bathrooms, reading-rooms, billiard-rooms, the hall, the bar, all the apparently obvious component parts of the big hotel are English importations adapted to English habits and made their way through the efforts of English visitors ? So much so that England's own hotels have taken a back seat, as the Continent grows *plus royaliste que le roi*, more English than England. Men's clothes all over the world follow London as a matter of course ; the whole of Europe has afternoon tea as a matter of course ; one dresses for dinner as a matter of course, as one has one's bath in the morning ; everybody has his English club armchair, drinks whisky, smokes Abdullas or Philip Morrises or a short pipe, plays his game of bridge, takes his English week-end off, visits the watering-places which the English, who discovered them, inhabit, has his office in the city and his club—in short conducts his whole existence *à l'anglaise*. That is how things stand in Berlin, as in Rome, Paris or Buenos Aires ; it is the triumph of England all along the line.

Let no one say that these are surface phenomena, a matter of fashion and snobbery, or that we are only here concerned with the customs of the upper classes (which is to-day synonymous with 'the rich') by whom the great masses remain unaffected. Hotels de luxe, golf clubs and the rest of it are only attainable by a few, but they are constituent parts of the ideal of all. The great masses always nourish the idea of having as good a time as the ruling class, and that class's way of having a good time always serves them as a model. The English ideal, which is a mixture of comfort, smartness, sport and open-air life, is the universal ideal to-day because it seems the most attainable one—is there at present a single reigning Royal Family that lives in any other way ? It has ousted all others, killing the French ideal of the *salon* and the *boudoir* and *esprit* in France, the German ideal of the officer and the ideal of the Bohemian artist. It has its advantages in hygiene, health and greater naturalness, its darker sides in the triumph of the physical over the mental, of form over content ; but its qualities and its defects are alike past discussion now. English ideas of conducting life have ousted all rivals ; from the millionaire's yacht in the Mediterranean to the Young Communist's football club, from the super-palace to the humblest middle-class week-end cottage, from the *Grande Semaine* at Deauville to the reception given by the mayor of a Balkan town, from the appointments of a millionaire's or a royal palace to the w.c. in a workman's dwelling, everything is stamped with an invisible mark, ' Made in England ' ; and whether one admires or despises these English forms makes no difference to the fact of their supremacy.

It is a fact which only enters the consciousness of a few people ; for, paradoxical as it may seem, at a time when everything is English England is as good as forgotten on the Continent. Europe's gaze is riveted on America to-day ; this is particularly the case in Germany, but to a greater or less degree in all continental countries : England, on the contrary, now as much as ever, sees in America a colonial country to whose independent development it takes up a rather critical attitude. In addition to its preponderating financial and economic influence on the Continent of Europe, America exercises a cultural—or anti-cultural— influence too ; its sky-scrapers and jazz-bands, films and cocktails, its passion for records and sensations, its methods of publicity and its ' hustle ' get enthusiastically taken up and copied. England has certainly not remained unaffected by American influence, but the Englishman instinctively resists Americanization, whereas people in Germany yearn towards it.

England's position in regard to America is quite different from that of the continental countries. Her influence on America is still stronger to-day than America's on her; for America's roots are in England and she will never rid herself of this historical and cultural heredity; on the other hand the things England takes from America do not go beyond the surface. But the Continent stares with envious admiration at the wealth and progressiveness of the United States and thinks to find salvation in the American gospel, in so far as it does not seek it in Moscow. The worshippers of technical achievement, capitalism and wealth aim at Americanization, the apostles of social justice and the Dictatorship of the Proletariat at Bolshevization; neither party, however, understands England or sympathizes with her. The 'American' party regard England as a sort of preliminary step to the United States, an old-fashioned concern that has got left behind and stuck half way; the 'Russian' party see in it a reactionary oligarchy. England, which a short time ago still passed for the most progressive of countries, now passes for the most reactionary, just as it did in Napoleon's days and with just as little justification.

Since the War England has been going her own way more than ever, and that way has been taking her far from the Continent: she has become almost a stranger to Europe, while Europe has almost dropped out of her field of view. The War and the events following it have led to prodigious revolutions, external and internal, on the Continent, in which England has taken no part. In spite of all the hatred and all the quarrels between the continental nations the War and its aftermath have drawn them together and made them much more like each other ; they have a common destiny but England has its own, and that is the deep ground of their mutual estrangement. The importance of England is to-day greatly under-rated on the Continent, and the part she plays in the world is not understood. It is not the first time in history that this has been the case, and this time too things will change. England is not a part of Europe but she is not a poor relation of the United States either nor does the negative fact that she is the enemy of Bolshevism by any means exhaust her significance. England is now, as she has been in the past, of the greatest consequence for mankind ; she has her aims and her tasks, in fact, she stands for something. To find the answer to the question, What does England signify to-day ? one must broaden one's horizon and contemplate not England and the continent of Europe but the British Empire and our whole planet—the only angle of vision from which it is possible to perceive what the upshot, to date, of the long march of English history is and what its significance and message for mankind.

CONCLUSION

ROUGHLY a fourth part of the surface of the globe and a fourth part of the earth's inhabitants are under British rule. The British Empire is the largest that the world has seen, also the most complex and difficult to understand. It is not geographically coherent, as the Roman Empire was and the Russian and American dominions are to-day, nor does it any longer consist as it once did of a mother country and her colonies; it is an absolutely unprecedented and unique thing. All other vast empires have been or are unified, centralized, territorially coherent, with a centre and a circumference, in a word, logical formations, whereas the British Empire is incoherent, illogical and to all appearance haphazard. The English jest mentioned before, to the effect that the Empire was created in a fit of absent-mindedness, contains a part, though not the whole, of the truth. It is just the unsystematic, illogical, apparently haphazard quality that is the really English thing about this organism, which has come into existence instinctively and grown up like a forest and is a natural product not made with hands. It has no hard and fast form and, strictly speaking, no constitution; in fact, strictly speaking, there is no Empire at all, the term being only a makeshift; for the King of England is sovereign of the Dominions beyond the Seas, Emperor of India and so on, and there is no name for the whole structure. It bears the truly English stamp of the natural growth into which Reason has only introduced some degree of order as an afterthought, thus representing the exact antithesis of the systematic conquests of Napoleon.

The English genius is intuitive and the British Empire a chaos, like the works of Shakespear or like its metropolis, London; but side by side with this intuitive creativeness the Englishman has a practical sense, which does not act according to logic either but enables him to find solutions without over-much cudgelling of his brains to the innumerable problems which the control of this vast Empire involves and to which no logical mind acting according to principles would be equal. The Englishman understands the art of letting things and people grow and only interfering in their development when necessary: just as the English park, in contrast to the geometrical French kind, is nature, i.e. nature emended and shown the way it should go, so is this Empire an organism that has formed naturally. Being a living thing, it is in the throes of perpetual change; it grows in one place and crumbles away in another, like the coast of the British Isles. Life, which means struggle ending in victory or defeat, the chances of the voyage of discovery or the trading expedition, in a never-ending process of development builds up this entity, which is never fixed and never takes on a definite form, because it would then grow rigid and die. It is always struggling, always threatened in one or more places, never secure, because life is a perpetual struggle, and its development is always startling and unforeseen, probably even by the directors of its destinies.

Consider the results of the World War. England was fighting for Belgian neutrality—in other words, for the security of the Flanders Coast—and for the command of the sea, against German commercial competition and lust for hegemony. To-day the British Empire has stronger rivals in sea-power and commerce and more of them; it has not achieved its own war-aims; but as if by accident, the War dropped Palestine and Mesopotamia into its lap. Egypt, Arabia and Mesopotamia are to-day connected by railways and motor roads, and the overland route to India is almost complete ; a vast wedge of territories under British rule (which has many forms and many names) extends from Cairo to India, and there is now a continuous chain of British possessions from the Cape to Cairo. Certainly no English statesman foresaw these developments in 1914 or consciously furthered them ; they came as a surprise and are hardly grasped even to-day.

The British Empire is in the middle of a process of transformation. The last Imperial Conference—these meetings of the prime ministers of the countries of the British Empire, which characteristically take place at irregular intervals, constitute the only institution that could be described as an imperial government—framed a number of resolutions which take account of the changed conditions, in other words, in a true English fashion gave its retrospective sanction to existing facts. The main point is this : the British Empire is bigger and more powerful than ever, but the centre of gravity has shifted, leaving the position of the mother country within the Empire weaker. As so often before in the history of the Empire, the immediate task is to take the altered conditions into account and find a formula which roughly corresponds to the facts to-day—nobody will imagine that it is intended to last for ever. That is the English way of bringing order into chaos and regulating the natural park a bit, it is the practical sense which makes the intuitive creation serviceable for the time being.

The British Empire is haphazard and without plan, but the last thing it is is meaningless. It is an expression of the English nature and of English ideals and can count on certain deep and unchanging convictions which permeate every manifestation of the English spirit. I have attempted in this book to investigate these characteristic features of the English nature in many spheres, alike in social life and town-planning, in literature and education, in politics and sport, and to demonstrate that the guiding lines are everywhere the same and never consciously realized. The British Empire is an expression of the same ideal that is responsible for, let us say, the University of Oxford, Society, the parliamentary system and the architecture of London—its grandest, most comprehensive and most universally significant expression, which embraces everything that I have said about certain individual phenomena of English life and everything that could be said about so many others that I have passed over; it is the living symbol of a philosophy of life.

England believes in the ideal of freedom but not in the ideal of equality. Nature knows nothing of equality. The Englishman, being an individualist both for himself and for other people, on the one hand considers unfettered development a worthy object of ambition and on the other believes in a hierarchy of human beings. That is what makes him aristocratical and a breeder of aristocracies of every kind: he breeds human beings just as he breeds race-horses and roses, and according to his instinctive conviction one can no more put human beings on the same level than one would a race-horse and a cart-horse or a dog-rose and a *Maréchal Niel*— a conviction which is not peculiar to those on whom Fortune has smiled but is also nourished by those whose lot is cast in dark places. It is this that makes England breed aristocrats and submit to their rule. Every gardener knows that one can only get outstandingly large and beautiful flowers or fruit by sacrificing numbers, that one has to choose between quality and quantity: England has chosen quality; but in so doing—and this distinguishes it from other aristocracies—it knows how to soften things down and arrive at compromises, having no rigid principles but merely instinctive inclinations which are kept in check by practical sense. Its aristocratic structure is elastic; the basis is always being broadened, new blood gets admitted and the conditions of the time are reckoned with; in a word, liberty reduces inequality and the aristocracy has certain democratic features.

All these tendencies re-appear in the British Empire. The Empire is governed by the mother country in the same manner as England is by a tolerant aristocracy open to new ideas. The English are the aristocrats among the subjects of the Crown, but they have learnt that this aristocracy has got to be inclusive and not exclusive—a thing they have not always known, or the United States would still be a part of the Empire. The loss of America has the same significance in the history of the Empire as the execution of Charles I has in the history of the English monarchy—namely, the bankruptcy of Absolutism, as a single warning decisive for all time to come. Parallel with the gradual broadening of the aristocracy's basis and the disappearance or further extension of privileges runs the broadening of the basis of the Imperial aristocracy. First in order come the 'white' countries of English settlers. Starting from isolated settlements they got welded into unities, which have gradually increased in independence, approximating more and more to the position of the mother country, and achieved equality of rights—have been admitted into the ranks of the aristocracy, in fact. Such has been the development of Canada, Australia, the Union of South Africa, New Zealand, Newfoundland and, recently, Ireland; the last example, i.e. the Irish Free States as a constituent part of the British Empire, being in the highest degree characteristic of the English. These countries are completely independent fiscally, and such contributions as they make (in these days) to the cost of Imperial Defence are voluntary. They have their own parliaments and make their own laws ; the English Governor, who represents the King, possesses a theoretical right of veto which he no more puts into practice than the King himself does his theoretical statutory powers. Since the latest resolutions of the Imperial Conference, which have been confirmed by a change in the title of the Sovereign, they are now only held together by a personal tie connecting them with the person of the Sovereign, i.e. they are colleagues of the mother country and hence also have a hand in determining British foreign policy. Their cohesion to-day is voluntary, like that of a family in which the grown-up sons are independent and have equal rights with the old man but accord him the primacy to which his age entitles him : this family of nations reminds one of the family policy of the House of Rothschild.

The above-mentioned Dominions may to-day be completely on an equality, but this is not the case with all the other possessions subject to the Crown ; their degrees of independence or, if you like, subjection, are very various, graduated and adjusted to the circumstances. The West Indies, Ceylon and Gibraltar, for instance, are governed by a Council nominated by the Governor, and one or two African possessions are entirely under the control of the Governor; but a gradual advance towards self-government is taking place everywhere, and the ideal of the central government is to make them all self-supporting, self-defending and self-governing. They all have their own budgets and their own representatives, in contrast to the French system which puts colonial administration under the control of the

French parliament and sends French Deputies for the Colonies to the Chamber. Then again there are the Protectorates, spheres of influence and, nowadays, the Mandated Territories like Palestine and Mesopotamia, which stand in another, looser relation to the Empire. Finally there is India, the Empire's most important possession and its most troublesome one, which enjoys a quite peculiar position. India is an Empire since Disraeli's revival of this title of the Mogul dynasty and the coronation of Queen Victoria as Empress of India ; nevertheless it is not by any means a homogeneous structure but an exceedingly complex one. It is represented by a Secretary of State for India, who is a Cabinet Minister, and the Crown is represented in it by the Viceroy, who presides over the Council of India, which is more and more adopting the forms and powers of a parliament and consists of an upper and a lower chamber. Alongside of British India, however, there are the Independent States, which are all in fact more or less independent. India is neither nationally nor religiously united—the dissensions between Hindus and Mohammedans are its greatest weakness—and it is not to England's interest to bring this union about. India is one of the great resources of the Empire and the English are putting off the granting of Dominion status : the Indians are coloured people, and the coloured man's relation to the white man is that of an inferior—that is the conviction of every individual Englishman and a fundamental axiom of British rule. Coloured people do not belong to the 'aristocracy' and they are not to be let in to it, if it can be avoided ; but if it cannot, England will find herself face to face with a new problem. It is impossible to prophesy what the solution will be ; one can only say that in all probability a compromise will be found or at any rate sought: for the present, however, the Indians belong to the second class of British subjects. The third class are the Negroes. The importance of Africa for the British Empire is increasing, and it may be that a single vast Dominion will come into existence there ; in the meantime England is developing the rich potentialities of the Sudan, which might possibly in many respects take the place of India.

This short and highly incomplete survey of the structure of the British Empire is enough to explain its prodigious many-sidedness and to throw light on the main outlines of the way in which this gigantic complex is administered ; but what is its value and its significance for England, and further, its significance for Europe and for Humanity ? Neither question is a simple one to answer. From the point of view of the State, England's colonial possessions are a source of great burdens as well as advantages to her ; she draws no direct revenues from the Colonies in the form of taxation, but she builds roads, railways, schools and churches in them ; in addition to that, many of the daughter countries have developed into competitors of their mother country, and the competition among them themselves is even keener. The State reaps no direct material advantages, and so far, at least, every attempt at a closer economic bond has come to grief ; the economic unity of the Empire has never materialized and in most cases neither English goods nor English settlers get preferential treatment.

All the same, England's wealth is based on her colonies. English capital builds the railways, keeps the steamship-lines going, finances the mines and plantations and draws vast dividends from them. The Colonies constitute a staple market for English goods even without Preference, the less independent ones, like India, being often closed to foreign competition ; and from these revenues great sums in turn flow into the Exchequer in the form of taxes. Certain classes of the community derive immense advantages from the existence of the Colonies, others lose by it—the farmers, for instance. It is, however, perhaps questionable whether the same result would not be achieved even without English suzerainty, as long as trade and industry flourished ; for every country that is in a position to export capital and invest it in foreign or overseas enterprises makes money out of the countries in which it invests, as witness France before the War and the United States since ; and the trade, the industry and even the politics of the debtor state get into the hands of the creditor. Hence to-day, when England's trade and industry are having to face competition everywhere, the importance of a closer bond with the Empire is far greater than it was before the War, and the development of England away from Europe again links up with this. Instead of the colonies' being dependent on the mother country, the mother country is gradually becoming dependent on the colonies. England has declined in relative importance while the Empire has increased ; the centre of gravity is shifting from the centre to the circumference, and it is possible that even the centre will shift ; Bernard Shaw in one of his plays which deal with the future, *Back to Methuselah*, makes Baghdad the future metropolis of the British Empire, and though that looks like a paradox, it is not so impossible. The strength of the British Empire lies in its power of transforming and adapting itself, which is contingent upon the looseness of its form. England has no great future before her apart from the Empire ; the maintenance of it is vital to her and constitutes the chief problem of British policy. The mother country can never by her unaided efforts re-conquer the position of supremacy she has lost ; for the loss was due not to a decline in her own powers but to the increased strength of the competition, especially that of the United States. England's rise to power was based on the start got by her industrial development, in which she was fifty years ahead of the rest of the world ; she stood alone but stands alone no longer and will never do so again. If she were merely a European commercial and industrial country there is no question that she would inevitably be reduced to the third or fourth place ; but she is the head of the British Empire. Will she be able to maintain that Empire ? Is she strong enough to do it ?

The end of the Empire, its disintegration, has often been prophesied and often announced as already on the way. Before the War, in Germany among other places, people nourished the illusion that on the outbreak of War the ' Colonies ' would break away ; instead of which they rushed to the support of their mother country. To-day people see the Empire threatened in many places and conclude that the end is near : China is in an uproar, in India attempts at revolution are chronic, Egypt is in a ferment, they are attacking the Union Jack in South Africa. But this vast Empire has been in a constant state of being threatened in one or more places right through its history, without thereby going under ; the prophets who announce its end fail to grasp its fundamental conditions, its elasticity and the really deep roots of its power. Possibly China—i.e. the Chinese market—is as lost, and not to England alone, of course; India will probably sooner or later throw off English control ; but meantime a new Empire is growing up under British suzerainty in Mesopotamia, Palestine and Arabia, and the Sudan, in itself a prodigiously rich country, gives England control over Egypt through the Assuan dam, in spite of the fact that Egypt has become an ' independent ' state.

It is, however, above all, the ' white ' countries,

Australia, South Africa and Canada, which have all the potentialities in them for turning into Americas someday, that are coming on in an unprecedented way. But will they not declare their independence, just like America ? The answer to this question about the future is to be found in their development up to now. England has governed her realm wisely, apart from certain isolated cases which have been fully avenged, like her blunders in dealing with Ireland and America. Instead of plundering and oppressing the subject countries, she has tried to educate them up to independence and not continued her 'aristocratic' methods longer than was wise ; she has known how to give way when it was necessary and had the wisdom to give the daughter countries a stake in the interests and the prosperity of their mother-land ; she has never fallen into the error of centralization and unification, never required her subjects to adopt English manners and habits, religion or traditions ; in short, she has avoided all coercion, or at least kept it down to a minimum, and that is the foundation of her present strength.

No conceivable force of arms could enable England to coerce her 400,000,000 subjects beyond the seas into obedience ; the British Empire can only hold together if it wants to hold together ; it must be a voluntary union or nothing ; but its significance and its lesson to the world lie in the proof it has given that such a union is possible. Resting not on force of arms but on the force of ideas, it is unshakable as long as the idea is alive. Its weak points are those where force is necessary, like India ; its strong ones those where the mother country has no force at its disposal, that is, in the ' white ' Dominions ; the link with these is unbreakable, but the link with the other parts of the Empire will only last until they prefer someone else's rule to England's. The moment for this does not, however, seem to me to be so near as is often supposed. Generally speaking, English administration in the coloured colonies is just, and the natives have sense enough to appreciate this fact ; they prefer the rule of the English to that of other white races and mostly have more confidence in British justice than in that of their own people. The English ideal has established itself practically everywhere and the peoples are not opposed to it ; what upsets them is the slighting attitude of the Whites towards the coloured people ; they do not so much want to get rid of their rulers as to enjoy equal rights with them ; in fact, they would like to work their way up into the aristocracy. How long England's suzerainty over the coloured colonies lasts depends on her handling of this problem.

Until a few years ago the coloured world knew of no ideal but the English, and all its aspirations were directed towards developing on English lines and attaining to parliamentary government, freedom of the press and the election of its own representatives. This fact constituted the real triumph of England, which was the triumph of the English ideal, and the real question is, Will this ideal retain its powers of attraction and conquest ? What really matters is not whether a country nominally forms part of the British Empire, but whether the spirit of England is supreme in it ; for it s this spiritual bond in the long run that alone can hold the Empire together. From this knowledge springs England's hostility to Bolshevism. For the first time since England started governing coloured peoples, another and opposite gospel is making its way to them from Europe, and the idea of the Dictatorship of the Proletariat is setting itself up against the idea of aristocracy. England must fight it, for it is the negation of everything English.

Let us make a summary of the things we have come to recognize as English. England is individualistic, convinced of the inequality of individuals and races, and hence believes in the aristocratic principle and the hierarchical structure of society, and for that reason also in toleration, which is the recognition of inequalities, in individual liberty and in justice, which respects all divergences. England's social structure, her government and the British Empire all rest on this view of life, its exponents are to-day supreme over a quarter of the globe; and the tenets of communism are its negation.

Communism represents the equalizing, levelling principle; it knows nothing of liberty or toleration and in principle sees justice in the government of all by all. It is a gospel which sounds fascinating to the 'people of the second order' in every country of Europe and to all who are not numbered among the aristocracy, but still more fascinating to the coloured races, who have never once till now had the possibility of equal rights and equal status held out to them. It is a new gospel, not unlike the Christian Gospel in its tenets (its practice is irrelevant here), just as the English gospel has many analogies with the Roman. This is no place to examine the question which ideal is higher or better, and anyhow there is no possibility of coming to an objective decision; some people accept the teaching of Christianity as the summit of all virtue and the following of it as the most worthy of all aims; others consider it a 'slave morality' that would fain destroy everything of value. The object here is not to pass judgment on them but to show their probable consequences. The introduction of communism into the coloured countries and the triumph of its doctrines means the end of the hegemony of the white race; it means the loss of all colonies outside Europe, equality of status for the coloured worker and consequently the reduction of the standard of life to a bare minimum, at least until there is a world state exempt from all competition ; it means the transformation of the countries which attract immigrants—America, Australia and South Africa—into coloured countries ; it means the equality of all individuals and all races, and that means for the White Man a decline into the insignificant position which on the score of numbers belongs to him. The first thing communism does—and is bound to do—inside a country is to annihilate the ' aristocracy ' ; and it would annihilate the ' aristocracy ' of the white races in just the same way. To-day England is the champion of this ' white aristocracy,' this hegemony of the white minority over the great coloured majority.

The British Empire is to-day a necessity to England ; its importance for Europe lies in the fact that it is the champion of the world supremacy of the White Man. There is nothing more short-sighted than the belief that any European country whatever could benefit by a weakening of the British Empire ; certain commercial interests might derive some transient advantage from it, but the supremacy of the White Man depends on England and would disappear with her. Even the United States would be unable to arrest this process ; the future of the British Empire is the future of the white race. England forms the natural link between white Europe and white America, being geographically nearer to the former and spiritually to the latter ; together they make up the white race which in the last few centuries has imposed its sway on the entire globe, and the leader of the conquering Whites has long been England and is still to-day the British Empire. Europe has been weakened and split by the breaking away of Russia ; the United States are self-enclosed and busy with their own affairs—in other words, powerful as they may be, in relation to world politics they are provincial ; the champion of the White Man is the British Empire. Whether it will win only the future can show. There are some serious opponents of the White Man in his own camp. The general tendency since the War is against English ideas ; people have been moving away, either to the Right or to the Left, from parliamentary government, Liberal traditions, and Free Trade. Neither Communists nor Fascists have sentimental feelings about the liberty of the individual, the free expression of opinion, or toleration. The idea of the Gentleman and education in independence and self-control are aristocratical and individualistic aims which run counter to the mass- and machine-age. Even in England the numbers of those who are opposed to what I have here described as the English ideal are high ; American mechanization and standardization are in their outcome more akin to the products of communist government than to those of the English tradition, and they find admirers and imitators in every country of Europe. In short, the English ideal is considered old-fashioned and out of date. It may be that its day is over, but I do not think so : other countries have often in the past apparently left England behind by a sudden jump forward, but a little time showed that this development by jerks had no permanence, and there was England, which had been plodding steadily on, ahead once more !

One thing is certain : the British Empire will last just as long as its spiritual basis remains a living and effective force and no longer ; but the end of it will also be the end of the world-wide rule of the White Man.

The intention of this book is to throw light on the character of a nation and an Empire whose significance for Humanity is overwhelmingly great. They are far too little known, and if this book contributes in any degree, however small, to the spread of a knowledge of them, it will have fulfilled its purpose. That this contribution is necessarily very incomplete follows obviously from the bigness of the theme, and the subjective nature of the judgments it contains is no less unavoidable ; but the author's object has been neither to praise nor to find fault but to explain. One may condemn England and all she means to the world or one may praise them to the skies, one may feel liking or antipathy towards her, but one must not overlook her ; love or hatred makes no difference to the fact that her future is of the greatest consequence for the whole of Humanity. That is why one must try to understand her, to reduce the contradictions which her ambiguous nature involves to a common denominator, and to get to know the main guiding lines of her development from her commercial and political life, from her history and from the climatic and geographical conditions which have made the English race what it is, and grasp their inner meaning. That this book may contribute to that end is the desire and intention of its author.